The Musical Life

ALSO BY W. A. MATHIEU

———

The Listening Book: Discovering Your Own Music

The Musical Life

REFLECTIONS ON

WHAT IT IS AND

HOW TO LIVE IT

W. A. Mathieu

SHAMBHALA
BOSTON & LONDON
1994

Shambhala Publications, Inc.
Horticultural Hall
300 Massachusetts Avenue
Boston, Massachusetts 02115

9   8   7   6   5   4   3   2   1

First Edition

Printed in the United States of America on acid-free paper ⊗

Distributed in the United States by Random House, Inc., and in Canada
by Random House of Canada Ltd

Library of Congress Cataloging-in-Publication Data

Mathieu, W. A.
The musical life: reflections on what it is and how to live it/
W. A. Mathieu.—1st ed.
p.   cm.
ISBN 0-87773-670-7
1. Music—Philosophy and aesthetics.   I. Title.
ML3845.M382   1994   93–39776
781—dc20   CIP
                            MN

To my parents
Aron and Rosella

Contents

Preface   xi

1. LIFE MUSIC

Shower Hero   3
Everyday Rhythm   6
Everyday Pitch   9
Bug on a Tamboura   10
Boundary Events   13
Electric Bridge   18
First World Piece   21
The Mind of Sound   24

2. MUSIC AND WORDS

Music versus Words   29
Listening to Evening   32
When Cousins Fall in Love   34
Paper Rope   38

3. SOUND SELF

Central Fish   41

Be a Movie   43

Ephemerals   45

Yawning Confession   47

Sound Apples   49

Sound Memory   51

Name History   54

Voice Mask   57

Inner Voice   60

Breathing Sound   62

Ultimate Mixer   64

4. THE MUSIC MIRROR

Some Music Mirrors   69

Simple Is Complex   74

Home   76

Memory Bin   80

Whatsa Matta wid da Bass?   85

"You Can't Do Anything Twice"   87

*Consonance and Dissonance (*No! No! No!*)*   90

Healing Music   95

Poison Music   97

Concert Music, Sky Music, Wedding Music   100

5. WHAT A COMPOSER DOES

Composition as Self-Expression   105
Craft   107
What Is It a Piece Of?   111
Discovery, Prophecy   116
Writing It   118
Pleasure in the Long Cycle   123
Erased Music   126
Fighting the Dead   129
Bach Dying   131
So That's What We Do   133

6. SOUND IS THE TEACHER: A FEELING FOR NUMBER

Abundance   139
Long Tones   141
Firefly Constellations   144
Human Unison   146
Composite Sound   152
Octave Mystery   154
The Rope Trick   156
Duple Nature   158
Weeny Person   161
Two Was Good   164

7. SOUND IS THE TEACHER: MUSIC APPEARS

Triple Nature   169

A House for Sound   173

The Powers That Be   175

Pentamerous Nature   178

Naming the Tones   183

Three Ways to Produce Overtones   192

String Ocean   197

Timbre Sauce   199

The Overtones as Musical Infrastructure   201

Our Harmonious Nature   205

8. HONEYSUCKLE BREATH

World Craziness   213

As If It Were Music   215

Honeysuckle Breath   217

Sources and Diversions   221

Discography   235

Preface

⸺⸺⸺⸺⸺⸺ ⁊ ⸺⸺⸺⸺⸺⸺

P EOPLE OFTEN ASK ME, with a kind of misty longing, "What's
it like to be a musician—to hear and think musically?"
There's a certain romance to this question, but underneath it lies
the statement *I don't have a musical nature; that is for others.* Yet
the truth is that musicality is as given as fingers and toes.

There are twin questions spinning through these essays:
What is musical? How can we use it? Being musical does not
necessarily mean being a musician; it doesn't mean playing the
piano at parties or composing songs for lovers. It is a way of
being awake, an angle of perception, a tilt of the ear. The musical
ear knows it is innately in tune with the universe. A person can
talk or move musically, or simply *be* harmonious without being
a fine violinist. You do not need a musician's craft to know that
both you and music are made from the same design.

How can I wake up to what I have? becomes the question,
not *How much do I have?* You have what you need. The folks
who convinced you that you don't "have it" are themselves
asleep to what is given in human form. Deep down everyone
knows that inside there is a vibrant musicality. Sometimes you
can feel it welling up and bursting out on its own. But how
can you purposefully draw this forward into the steps and
breaths of daily life?

The everyday part of us is more likely to have a flyswatter
in its hand than a violin. We are more likely to be walking

from the kitchen to the dining room not spilling soup than realizing the fine ballet we are performing. I want to point out the musical sense that is already in that life, just waiting for you to notice it, right there where it has been all along.

This recognition comes through willful listening—unobstructed and unencumbered, with no arm in the way and no wadded cotton either. We have the ability to discover what stops our ears and muffles our hearing; indeed, the obstructions themselves often turn into our best friends, like repressed memories that surface and turn into forgiveness.

ᵔ

Everybody has an idea about life. The mason says life is like laying bricks. The chef says it is a seven-course meal. Microbiologists say if we understand microbes we will understand ourselves. This book comes more from a feeling than an idea. It is the feeling I have in my own daily life as a composer and as a teacher, the buoyant complicity that comes from knowing sound.

This feeling can't be said, of course, or written. But consider the faceted, compound eye of a moth: it sees the world through a thousand lenses. Each lens senses an incomplete blur, yet the moth's brain assembles the blurred messages into a single image it can use. Let this book be a compound ear, each paragraph a lens for sound, which your ears assemble into a new harmony.

1

Life Music

Shower Hero

S TEAM IS BILLOWING UP in the shower. I am lathered all over, circling in my thoughts and lost in the sound of white water. Suddenly my wife's scream pries open my mind. I fling aside the shower curtain and prepare to leap down from the trees but, balanced on one leg and dripping, I realize that Devi is actually practicing vocal exercises. The tones of the scale are rising and falling in precisely sculptured terraces; she's singing in full voice and sounding just terrific. Three seconds ago I was rescuing my love from a dire fate; now I am passively delighting in her musicality. A leaping torso has been summarily transformed into an appreciative ear. As I rinse myself off I realize how my instinctual response to danger— my wildness—has been civilized by tone and tune. One extreme has been replaced by another. I turn off the water and clean up the mess.

My mind frequently returns to this region between scream and scale, an attractive zone where opposites cross over. I want to know all about the mysterious boundary that demarcates wildness from civilization, raw experience from the refinement of art. I want to know the territory between the rescuer and the connoisseur so well that I can draw advantage from either, play one against the other, and live in the best of both of their worlds.

3

In my boyhood, each time I played Mozart for my Grandma Clara, she said, in a flat voice, "Sounds just like water." One day, on a picnic, she announced factually that the creek sounded just like Mozart.

Ten years ago, while visiting New York City, I witnessed a SoHo performance art piece that concluded with a twenty-minute movie of three brown cows grazing peacefully behind a wooden gate, much like the brown cows that graze behind the wooden gate across the road from my house in California. "For this I paid fourteen dollars?" I asked myself, and went back to California. Only when I saw the real cows across the real road did I consider how the movie cows might have been appreciated in Manhattan.

When you put a frame around something, it's a picture. An empty frame laid anywhere on the forest floor is nature art. Anything on TV is television. Any moment lifted out of time is a photograph. You pay to see movie cows. Art is frames and boxes, and we are always experimenting—framing this, framing that, placing this or that in boxes we invent and discard. These trials are good for us; they make us question which metaphors are useful and which are expiring from old age. They make us peer at our lives from many perspectives and examine that examining. "And tho' she feels as if she's in a play—she is anyway." That's from "Penny Lane," by John Lennon, who knew all about it.

Someone who is living a musical life may not necessarily hear the music of Mozart in a brook, but does hear, in the sound of the brook, a beauty that is kin to Mozart's music. There are times when that mysterious kinship is thrust upon you, like when you attempt a daring rescue of your wife from her vocal practices. Sometimes it is pointed up by a nicely placed frame or box. But most often it is nascent and un-named, an uncharted current coursing beneath our perceptions. We have to caress and cajole it up to the surface all by ourselves, the way hungry kittens encourage the flow of their mother's milk with the pads of their little paws. We have to squeeze and press the beauty from the world.

Everyday Rhythm

I'M FIXING TO WRITE my daughter a letter in longhand with a "rolling ball" type of pen—black, extra fine. For a moment I sit feeling an arc from Sebastopol, California, to Chicago, Illinois. I exhale, rock a little with my pulse, then take a deep breath. In one long motion I reach in back of me into an open box for a sheet of stationary, place precisely on my desk its bright crackling flatness, and adjust my arm to penmanship readiness, including some practice strokes just above where I will write the date. I write the date. The smooth strokes of my sleeve on the paper's surface, the sharper strokes of my handwriting, and the rolling of the metal ball all blend together. *Dear Amy.*

Now my thought rhythms mix with the sounds and motions of writing. *These birds, the light of this May afternoon, nothing to do but write, what are you doing now?* The patterns of my thoughts and actions are superimposed on my thoughts of her thoughts. The pen scrapes, the body rocks, our lives touch for a page of words. *Love, Dad.*

The envelope, the stamp, the ritual of gummy licks. Walk to the big blue mailbox, put up the flag for the mail lady. The falling cadence of an action finished—wrote it, mailed it—folds into the larger rhythm of the spring day. Next thing now.

For the living, time does not merely pass. It passes in spoonfuls and handfuls, lumps and parcels and slices. Sometimes time is wavy with crests and troughs like folded mountains. In the swing of domestic chores I am an object making waves in time, a skiff trailing a braided wake.

"Everyday rhythms" are these divisions of time, which we feel through the motions of walking, eating, and working; through gladness and sadness coming and going; through the forms of clouds and undulating hills, and the butterflies over them. Sometimes the rhythms are silent as the moon; others, like pulses of laughter, love the ear and remind us of music.

From apparent randomness, patterns emerge. You wash a dish and there is another dish to wash. You look up into the clouds and there are the long fingers of a hand. Nervousness in your own fingers becomes a catchy tap dance on the tabletop, bringing your mind back suddenly from some steep edge.

Such periodicities appear unbidden. They have inside them a nurturing energy that buoys us up, turns housecleaning into choreography and conversation into poetry. We have all but lost the tribal songs of work and the childhood songs of play, but they are still alive in the web of our days, waiting to be heard again.

Meter is the *equal* division of time. A steady, underlying meter measures the less regular rhythms passing above it, much as an even gait might measure the passing of cars and flying of birds and the flow of conversation that a walker walks through.

You could meter mere life by counting evenly to yourself a slow two-count while paying attention to what you see and hear. The weave of creation feels different that way. I want it to feel different. I want the scrubbing of the potatoes and the rising of the guests from chairs to be domestic epiphanies, the brushing of your teeth to be some new sort of samba. Even the bright and dark places in your feelings can be a kind of private shadow dancing. And the rhythms of your breath breathing and your eyes blinking could weave with the words and thoughts of these sentences into the music of some sweet little greeting dance.

Everyday Pitch

W HEN I STRIKE a wine glass with my fingernail I can feel the glassy sound in my brain. I can imagine the molecules of glass: a crystal lattice whose pattern rings out and spins forward like an arrow. I hitch a ride on the arrow.

By making the motion of striking the glass but not striking it—by *pretending* to strike the glass—I can hear the tone in my head. Now I strike the glass for real. Now I pretend to strike it, making real the internal sound. It *amazes* me that I can induce myself to hear this way.

It is one thing merely to hear a sound, quite another to register its pitch. The awareness of the pitch of a glass gives pleasure. That same pleasure can come to you naturally many times a day from unexpected sources: machines, furniture, utensils. As you develop sensitivity to pitched sounds, normal life takes on a glinting, melodious texture. It's as if you see for the first time the colored threads in an old shirt. A heart beats in dead matter. Plain stuff sings.

Ancient joke: Two hip dudes are walking down the street. A huge safe falls to the ground just behind them.

"*Man,* what was that?" says one.

"E flat," says the other.

Bug on a Tamboura

I WANT TO BE A DOG or a dolphin. I want to hear through my cat's ears, to sing whale songs while being a whale. Have you noticed how the birds on country roads linger past the last second before they dart away from death? So it seems to us. But to a swallow my car is a slow-gliding boat, and he lifts off with the leisure of a pelican.

Do the wing beats of a hummingbird feel to the hummingbird like the strokes of the oars feel to the oarsman? Does the peck of a woodpecker seem rapid to the woodpecker, or more like the driving of a nail to a carpenter?

To our ears, the call of a Swainson's thrush sounds like an ascending whistle, jaggedly disappearing. But when you hear it four times slower and two octaves lower (by slowing down a tape recording) it sounds like a virtuoso performance on a wooden flute, delirious with tonal patterns and timbral shading. At the high point of the song, at the last rise, the membranes in the thrush's voice box divide, producing two-part harmony that leaps the trees. I long to know what he actually hears. I want to know how it feels through my bird bones for my call to illuminate the air of my creek in the proper tempo of my bird life.

Every spring my music studio is populated by an orange-limned bug—not just any old insect, but a "true bug," a distinguished member of the order Hemiptera. Devi says you can tell by the shape of its wings, which are wide and allow for long hops. When not hopping, the bugs waddle and wiggle their antennae. They are *cute* bugs, modest, occasional, tidy, and discreet, and I ordinarily let them be. One day, while I was sitting cross-legged on the floor, singing and playing the tamboura, I noticed a small fellow inching toward me across the carpet. The tamboura is a four-stringed drone instrument with a very long neck attached to a large round gourd—all hollowness and resonance. I had laid the neck down horizontally on the floor in front of me, the gourd end on my right. On impulse, I scooped the bug off the carpet and placed him carefully, right side up, in the middle of the tamboura's neck. Now the four wire strings of the instrument were directly over his head and stretched out to either horizon, appearing to him, possibly, the way immense electric power cables appear to us. Sri Hemiptera was accepting of his new surroundings. With shameless stealth I pressed the tip of my plucking finger down upon the thickest of the strings, then abruptly releasing the pressure, let loose the full sound energy of the deepest tone. Earthquake! My victim windmilled over heaving ground, parachuted onto the rug, and panic-sprinted straight for safe drapes.

Earthquakes jolt about twice per second and can displace quite a few inches of landscape per jolt. Suddenly—and frighteningly—I knew how the bug felt, because Devi and I, as upper-deck spectators of game 3 of the 1989 World Series at Candlestick Park in San Francisco, had survived an earthquake during which we believed we would perish. Now Great C was an earthquake to a bug. I found him again and repeated the experiment. Sure enough, he started out calm as a pillow, then Mayday!

This morning I repeated the trick for a four-year-old boy

who shrieked with delight, not so much because we were torturing a bug, I think, but because he also felt the vibration the
way the bug did. That momentary release from one form into
another is liberation. We laugh when we are suddenly free.

Poor bug.

When I am with animals, I try to listen through their ears
so as to hear their language as meaningful and ours as strange,
and to perceive with new ears sounds that are common and
familiar to humans. To bats, the whistle of a teakettle is a tuba.
Bats can teach you small music. If you could be the earth itself,
earthquakes would be silvery shivers. The planet can teach you
what it's like to be huge. Why be trapped in human form?
Wherever you can imagine to listen, there is music in that
dimension.

Boundary Events

I'M NOT SURE where music starts or where it ends, if it ever ends, but what is *musical* lives on the boundary of music, picking up music's accents and mimicking its manners. The boundary may shift around, but it is always a pleasant place, remindful of some forgotten goodness.

Here are some common events that take place on the boundary of music.

LAUGHING

When you laugh, the little I-give-up spasms in your diaphragm puff neat packages of air upward through your vocal cords and out into the world as discrete musical pitches. Hence the joy of abandon and the precision of music rise up together. Everyone has this little bit of music in their laughing.

TOASTING

When I clink wine glasses in a toast with someone, I hold my glass gently by the stem, not the bowl above the stem, and encourage my dining partners to do likewise. Then, instead of the usual sounds of *tuk* and *plink,* the rims will vibrate freely like the glass chimes they are and highlight the scene. At our house this happens as a homey ritual just after the dinner grace, allowing the whole day to flow singing through that one note.

FLINGING

I am always on the lookout for anything small that makes a good sound when flung down. Any old metal trash will do: washers, nuts, screws, bolts. Pennies do best.

It is not enough, picking up these objects, to jiggle or twirl them or toss them end over end. Nor is it sufficient to deduce from them or impute to them some scandal, or through their agency to speculate on the nature of chance or synchronicity. What is necessary is to cast them with decisive gestures onto the hard pavement. Pennies especially must be hurled and spun so they sail and skip, singing, out of sight. While setting their bodies free, we liberate their sounds, and there is hardly a sound anywhere so satisfying as the escape tone of a found object.

TALKING ON HOLD

We can talk faster than we think, most of us; typically the tongue has to wait more or less patiently for the brain to catch up. In order to caulk and mortar together our broken sentences, an unconscious and surprisingly musical language of *uh*s, *ah*s, and *mm*s arises. I've often thought to splice out these half-sung pitches from a tape recording of some dreadful lecture, and string them together into a kind of piece—a music made entirely from these orphans abandoned in the crevasses of speech.

But I don't really need a tape recorder to do this, just a shift in my hearing. Instead of waiting for someone's thoughts to come into focus, I can fuzz out the words and concentrate instead on those connective vowels and hums. Each one has an expressive tone; in sequence they become melodic; altogether they take on a kind of poignancy. "Keep listening," they say, "don't go away; hold on, my mind will catch up, I promise, I do, it will; keep listening, stay with me."

SINGING IN A CROWD

In a crowd I put a finger in my ear and sing or hum a few private notes to myself. My bones carry the message. I hear the crowd, the crowd does not hear me. Me and my voice, alone among many.

RADIO PEOPLE

Before we learned to structure the world through pixels on a screen, we learned to imagine it through our ears. The pre-TV generation raised during the Golden Age of Radio still has special ears attached to special eyes. Footsteps, doors, and wind are what life is made of.

Radio people are professional listeners, and they have tamed and trained their desire to be understood. Their voices know a thousand ways to catch your ear. Their energy is so concentrated on the sound of speech that meaning becomes clarified and heightened, and language becomes mellifluous.

You can listen to radio people as they listen to themselves. You can follow the flow of sound through the sensitivity of their ears, the musical rise and fall of their voices during the weather report or the sportscast.

One day recently, Hank Greenwald, who calls the play-by-play radio broadcast for the San Francisco Giants, allowed as to how, while eating crunchy fried chicken at lunch, he had been reminded of the European armies of World War II marching across the snow.

GROUNDING

We are used to sound in air. But sound also travels through water and earth, wood and metal. Recordings of whale and porpoise songs reveal an underwater world. But where are the mole and ant recordings? The footstep collections?

When I put my ear to the ground I can hear through the earth what could never be heard through the air. When I make a seal between my ear and the flat wall, I can hear the messages that beams carry between the foundation and the roof.

Through water, sound travels five times faster than through air; through metal, ten times faster. If I lay down my head and listen to my desk, or in the bath press my ear to the side of the tub, I can enter into the denseness and the quickness, the unfamiliar sounds of the familiar world.

CLOSING A DOOR

A door closes. It is a downbeat in local time. What part of life has just dropped off to the left; what has spilled to the right over the sill?

I go back and close the door deliberately, with analytical ears. What is the sound of the hinge, the insulation strip against the floor, the latch tongue being forced in, the latch tongue snapping out, the long wooden rectilinear edges meeting the rigid frame? A swinging door and what stops doors have collided. It is finished.

I do it again.

Electric Bridge

PERSONALLY, I HAVE TROUBLE with electronic music. To me, any music that isn't live and acoustic begins to sound, sooner than later, like the cardboard it's coming from. But there is a great value to electronic music often overlooked by such curmudgeons as I. It has to do with how we make music in the first place. Music is created, for the most part, by fooling with stuff, by trying things out, by plain old-fashioned screwing around. Never before have hungry, young musicians had so many toys with which to screw around in so many ways.

If the process of creating electronic music produces few fine violinists, it nevertheless engenders a new awareness of the nature of sound and of our responses to it. In each new experiment, the dynamic between life and its musical reflection is held up to scrutiny. Through new lenses we understand the sky in a new way. In different mirrors we look different. Music with new boundaries makes us hear ourselves anew.

There is an electronic technology called *sampling* by which you record a sound digitally and then, by means of a computer, alter its properties. Sampling offers many ways to alter sound—from simple repetition to timbral surgery. Phillip Kent Bimstein, who lives in Springdale, Utah, interviewed his neighbor, Garland Hirschi, who runs a large dairy herd, about his cows. Mr. Bimstein recorded not only the interview but also the lowing and calling of the cows themselves. By sampling Mr. Hirschi's voice and the voices of the cows, and mixing them with electronically generated orchestral sounds, he created a cross between an interview, an idyllic tone poem for orchestra, an electronic etude, and a bovine cantata. The result, "Garland Hirschi's Cows," is one of the wittiest and most musically beautiful pieces I've heard. Thanks to new sampling techniques, the voices of man and cow, while retaining their original natures, have also become new rhythmic and tonal instruments.

Martin Swan, also an electronic composer, says in reference to a recent project,

> A significant number of my percussion sounds were actually samples of household objects. For example, one of the tracks has a muted, tuned African drum sound, which we did using plastic Coke bottles filled with some water, so that shifting the bottle after you hit it created a little pitch change. I created my favorite shaker sound using a box of Grape Nuts. . . .
>
> I do a lot of huge pitch shifts to see what it sounds like. If you've got these buttons on a sampler, you might as well press them and see what happens. When I'm just mucking about with the machine, I'll reverse things just as a matter of habit. Sometimes you get amazing results.
>
> What's wonderful about the sampler is the fact that you can create new sounds or modify existing ones to the point where they become completely unrecognizable and they are culturally detached—they don't have any reference.

Our friends down the street are concerned about the amount of time their eleven-year-old spends hunched over his computer, which is hooked up to a keyboard synthesizer, among other things. It is true that while Jeremy is in his room frittering away his youth playing with wires and black boxes, he is not practicing scales and learning Chopin like his parents did. It is also true that he is programming a way of getting from point A in his ear to point B in yours that his parents had no language for. Sometimes we need new bridges over old ground. Maybe Jeremy, who is so into the computer screen that he has forgotten to eat dinner, is building one now.

First World Piece

M Y "SYMPHONY OF PLACE" is the totality of sound I register in the here and now. When I am aware of all the
sound in the sphere around me, there is a completeness to my
experience—a piece-ness. The *place* of my symphony can be
circumscribed and local, or it can be far-flung even beyond
my senses. For instance, when I listen to music in headphones,
physical place is bounded by the geography between my ears.
The horizon of sound is within my skull. This occurs also—
without headphones—just before dropping off to sleep, when
my mind, preparing its nest for the night, gathers up the universe.

Yet I can find myself walled in just as assuredly by the
exterior world, standing, for instance, on a noisy corner near
a construction site at rush hour. Monster machines, buses,
trucks, and sirens are in my face, compressing my sense of
place to a few cubic yards. Civilization is not always mean,
however. We have learned to share large spaces while
crammed together agreeably as bees: baseball parks where
large mobs, facing center, scream happily; and concert halls,
where we agree to listen quietly. There are even larger highly
populated soundscapes: from an overlook on the perimeter of
Hong Kong, the city at night sounds dulcet and benign.

As my sphere increases, my senses unfold. The rolling

fields of the country, the long hush of open water, are calming and expansive. In the mountains there seems to be no end to my perception. The pilot of a distant Cessna can't hear me, but I greet him anyway: hello, sky brother.

As you become more aware of soundscapes you can quilt them together. From separate movements, larger symphonies emerge. Sounds from the different rooms of a house become the sound of the house; the sounds of nearby streets become the sound of your neighborhood. You learn to recognize acoustic communities. You could draw a map of the sound sources and go "sound hearing" instead of sightseeing. As you travel, you realize how whole regions, entire cultures, have characteristic sound textures. American car horns, for example, are tuned a consonant third apart. In Asia, car horns are tuned a dissonant half step apart. In Muslim countries, boundaries are defined by the call to prayer, sung by the muezzin, whose voice is nowadays usually electronically amplified.

As your sense of place expands, your Symphony of Place becomes more inclusive. Your personal ecology broadens, and your sense of history also; you begin to hear the sound of your collective self. You realize how you are shaped by the sound of your culture and your world, past and present, and you take responsibility for your contribution.

The sound of the world begins with your own two ears, centered in your personal space; but if you listen attentively enough, and live long enough, you can hear the whole globe. You listen locally and hear globally. You take it all on.

Someday it will be time to make the First World Piece. My vision is that every last one of the billions of us will take up spoon and pot at the same moment and tap, beat, and bang a thanks to Mother Earth. Or maybe it will be a rolling composition, 24 hours of sunset rhythm, including vocals.

Man, woman, and child, everyone living, will be part of the same musical intention resounding around the world, a Yes Mass, a Global Symphony. Maybe it will be the first of many affirming actions by a united humanity. Won't that first one be grand?

The Mind of Sound

E VERYTHING IS ALIVE and singing, or nothing is. What we recognize as the vibrancy of our minds is at the heart of everything created, pervading and binding mice, minerals, and gravity. Each order vibrates in its fashion; every octave sings. Everywhere the oscillating flux is crooning its heart out.

Perhaps I am a tad crazy to believe this, a bit off the ecstatic deep end. But I teach music. I watch sound's spark light up the recognition in people's eyes during the magic moment of first hearing. I know life when I hear it. Sound, jostling and bashing us awake in the form of organized collisions of atoms of air, is nothing less than living mind.

Consider how a radio can be tuned to various frequencies in the electromagnetic spectrum: AM news, FM music, citizen's band cross talk, shortwave propaganda. Through each cubic jot of space courses a universe of coded waves waiting to be tuned into and decoded.

Our minds can be tuned to various levels of consciousness like a radio. The life energy of each realm has something to say. We can scan across the octaves and zero in on a particular energy and resonate with it, *get* some of it, skim off the cream. Painters are nourished by light, they feast on color; it's their dinner. Musicians eat sound. The extra nourishment you get from tuning in through your ears is food for your musical sensibilities.

The secret of the musical life is to be open to vibration at every level, to appreciate it wherever you find it. It is to be as at home among the configuring atoms as among the dervish galaxies, as among the waving, rustling grasses. The bare act of imagining these musics brings them forward for all to hear as surely as Mozart, imagining *his* music, brought it forward. His was an act of sheer will met by the universal will. Your tuning is an act of will also; but you don't have to be able to write or play such music, only to imagine it, or what it might be, for it to find you.

These imaginings are not focused, necessarily, on your ears. Use the part of you that leads through mazes and knows where to find fresh water and safe, dry houses. Thus a physicist, straining past all understanding to open the mystery of matter, learns to listen for quark music. What molecular biologist has not imagined DNA music? You can lie still in your room and hear room music. There exists, thus, spider music, moss music, cloud and thunderclap music, music of Gaia, and music of the spheres; any or all of these are sensible to saints and sinners. As ye are tuned, so ye shall hear.

Do not be surprised if, at the core of some such music, you find your own foggy fear, or your own loneliness. Or, at the flung edge of it, come up hopelessly lost. Gradually you learn how you yourself are a kindred one of those musics, one among many in a lavish opera. You are *made* of music—lonely music when you are lonely, vast music when you feel vast, even happy music sometimes. The whole stream of your life, already musical, is simply waiting for you to hear it.

2

Music and Words

Music versus Words

WE ARE BORN almost having language. It is so much a part of us that it is difficult to imagine life without it. But there are those moments of waking from a moody dream, those instants of total surprise or lighted eternities of lovemaking or absorption in music which seem both wordless and complete.

Words are *about* something, they signify what is outside themselves, and though they have their own innate being, that is not usually their essence. *Om,* yes. *Smack,* in a way. *Limpid,* possibly sort of. *Thermodynamics, function, consider,* no, no, no.

Utter wordlessness is the promise of pure music. The purpose of tone is to bring forward what is conscious without language, and to let it breathe slowly and deeply and safely in the present.

At some level, words require thought, and thinking can get a bad name. The Buddhist teacher Joe Miller said, "You can get more stinkin' from thinkin' than you can from drinkin'." Thinking is not the bad guy, of course, any more than vanilla pudding; problems arise when we do not consume our pudding in appropriate portions at proper times. Too much thought eclipses being. Discussing love is not love. Talking is not walking. Part of it, but not it.

I'm not saying what you don't already know, only what is easy to forget. It is easy to forget how words can be snakes, how they can hypnotize us into believing we are having experiences when we are only juggling ideas and rustling pages. Words can bring new vision into any moment, yes, but in that same moment they can cover our cage with a blanket.

When you do temporarily escape language you can go out on the wind like pollen. We are hungry for moments when the intellectual veil is lifted. We want to forget, "I think, therefore I am." We want *I am* or nothing.

Jelaluddin Rumi, most musical of poets, was also most chary of words and elegant in his longing to be free of them. Many of his poems end with an image meant to spring you free into silence:

> *Enough talking. If we eat too much greenery,*
> *we're going to smell like vegetables.*

> ᐓ

> *This talk is like stamping new coins. They pile up,*
> *while the real work is done outside*
> *by someone digging in the ground.*

> ᐓ

> *These words I'm saying so much begin to lose meaning:*
> *Existence, emptiness, mountain, straw:*
> *Words and what they try to say swept*
> *out the window, down the slant of the roof.*

> ᐓ

> *No more words. In the name of this place we drink in*
> *with our breathing, stay quiet like a flower.*
> *So the nightbirds will start singing.*

෨

A white flower grows in the quietness.
Let your tongue become that flower.

෨

A mouth is not for talking.
A mouth is for tasting this Sweetness.

Sometimes he is repelled by words, and his poetry seems exhausted. Even the images are too much:

If I could wake completely, I would say without speaking
why I'm ashamed of using words.

෨

I used to want a buyer for my words.
Now I wish someone would buy me away from words.
I'm so tired of what I've been doing.
Look for someone else to tend the shop.
I'm out of the image-making business.

Denial itself becomes burdensome, endangering the experience of wholeness:

You know this already, I'll stop.
Any direction you turn it's one vision.

But the beautiful words stream on anyway in a continual hunger. This same poem finishes with one more image: "my body is a candle touched with fire."

Poets *can't* stop.

Listening to Evening

L ET ME TELL YOU my big epiphany about language. I've
always been a musician—I've spent fifty years practicing
music. It never occurred to me to be a writer, option or no,
and only in the last five years have I tried to develop writing
discipline. The more I wrote and played with language, the
more absorbed I became in its delights and intrigues. At first
I fully anticipated being able to say what I mean, to so fill in
the *arteries* with word *blood* as to sense the *pulse* of the *heart*.
Or something. Perfect clarity does occur in music—one learns
to compose or perform all of what the moment carries, even
to spill some foam, so to speak. But I never feel that words
completely say what aches to be said.

Last year I was sitting on my studio porch doing my favorite thing: listening, after an afternoon of music, to the evening. Words drifted in and out of my mind, but mostly I was
hearing the evening song birds, the wind in the creek trees, a
little traffic, distant voices, and that fading hush that opens the
ears. All across the sky was the flickering between two worlds
(twilight means "two-light"). When I looked up, I felt a pulse
under my eyelids and thought, "I know this dusk flicker and
I'll bet everyone else does too, but there are just no words to
describe it. No way. Impossible."

Perhaps especially owing to the sweetness of the hour,

the inadequacy of language seemed like an abandonment, as though a good friend was letting me down. Then I found my-self remembering these words:

> *When the evening is spread out against the sky*
> *Like a patient etherized upon a table* . . .

I had been given ether as a child, I had been a patient etherized upon a table, had gone under and felt the twilight underneath. In adulthood I had read the T. S. Eliot poem many times. Now, as the childhood experience, the poem, and the present moment all came together, my love for language blossomed right there on the porch.

I saw that language is metaphor and simile, and that the operative word is *like,* spoken or implied. Words approach experience roundabout, pecking and jabbing at it from every side until eventually a blow draws blood, then a vital cut, then experience flows red. It is *like* that, and like *that,* till we zero in on meaning impossible to articulate directly. I began to enjoy this kind of play, even though it is more work than I bargained for. I began to appreciate the longing, in Rumi's poetry, to be filled with love and emptied of words. I began to understand how words that are beautifully right can bring you so close to the edge that all you have to do is make a little jump—plink!—like a finch off a wire.

Music is entirely specific: what you hear is what you get. Language is rich and various and inexact. You have to keep saying what is, a thousand ways, until someone jumps.

When Cousins Fall in Love

W HEN I WAS THREE YEARS OLD, deep in the safe sunny maples of southern Ohio, Great Britain was in the darkest time of World War II. Even though the grown-ups shielded us children from the war, we heard serious talk. We knew that our allies across the sea needed us desperately. Our childhood reached out to them. My nursery was next to the pantry, which contained the family refrigerator, a 1927 General Electric whose motor clearly said the word "England" when it turned on. Lying still in the early mornings, I would dream and wait. There!—it went "England." I found this intensely pleasurable. The refrigerator knew; its sound reached out to our friends, "England, hum hum hum, we won't let you die."

Children live close to the sound of words. We used to play a game: ask a grown-up to pick a word, any word— hatpin, or tabletop, or probable. Then we would repeat it ten hundred times—tabletop, tabletop, tabletop. Gasping and whooping, we would exorcise every last memory of meaning from the word until its sound emerged triumphant and we were helpless Jell-O. The grown-ups just didn't get it.

For writers it is easy to become obsessed with meaning, to follow it around as if it were the only light in the day. The opposite reaction is to be blindsided by the euphony of words, and to follow *that* self-consciously into the nether ether blabber blizzard weather. We want balance between sound and sense. It is expected (though not so often delivered) in poetry. I wish we readers of prose would more stridently demand it from others and from ourselves.

A similar problem exists for listeners of music. Concert music made for listening can be laden with meaning yet sound wretched. Paul Hindemith once said of an academic colleague, "His music sounds the way music ought to sound, but it doesn't sound like music." On the other hand, there is no scarcity of music that sounds wonderful but has the mind of a gnat. A few years ago, in an issue of *Billboard* magazine featuring New Age music, Nonesuch Records (which has an exemplary catalog of the world's finest music) ran a snipey ad that, centered on a full page and surrounded by white space, said, "YOU SPEND A THIRD OF YOUR LIFE ASLEEP. ISN'T THAT ENOUGH?"

The challenge for both listener and reader is to willfully seek balance between sound and sense, to sedulously insist on mind in music and euphony in language. Euphony is literally what is *well voiced*—pleasing sound. I like *Gatorade* and *pleasure, ebullient* and *punt,* and *rickshaw.* One's list should keep growing and changing.

Never stop listening to the rhythm of words. Read aloud, especially your own writing. Even letters. Even *memos.* If the rhythm isn't right, the writing isn't right. Words might mean a great deal even if their accents don't lope and sway and mesh, but not to me. If the rhythm doesn't gel, I just don't get it. I close the book, more willing to believe I'm stupid than read through dead sentences. When words swing, I'm smart.

Of course, you must say what you mean when you write and speak, but your meaning is deeper when your words are musical. Be like a child. Remember to hear words as nonsense, so the music in them will sound through. Then music and language will become allies who reach for each other over the great water and refuse to let each other die.

೦~

Music composition is, for me, more formal and precise than word writing. Usually there is a best way for a piece of music to be, and when you finally find it you say, "I've found it," and move on. Perhaps poets think this. But it is possible—probable—that you will wreck your prose if you mess with it long enough, even though it never seems quite perfect. You have to learn when to stop. From music I have learned an economy of means. The rule is: if it sounds too long, it is too long. If this means your six-page essay has shrunk to a pithy paragraph, tough potatoes and congratulations.

For me, music and words can be as havens from each other. When I am word-locked during the morning writing, one long tone can bring me back from blue to pink. And in the late evening, when I have become circumscribed and isolated by the music in my head, plain conversation will make me laugh again. Not surprisingly, rambling on in one medium tends to tighten up and sharpen the other. If I am working out a musical problem with tight tolerances, a gushy journal entry oils the tones. Likewise, nothing fixes stubborn sentences like rambling, uncritical musical improvisation.

೦~

Realization can be defined as fullness in the present. It seems perfect and natural for a musical tone or a drumbeat to be the agent of a realized moment, as natural as a kid's cry or a swung ax. Pure tones give pure guidance; and in a downbeat—the absolute union of Mother Earth and human body—there is absolute guidance also. In music, message and medium are allies wholly alloyed.

Yet realization can be just as true in the moment of writing; true in the content and in the quality of language. Your whole history has led to the present word—this word is the lead bird of the entire flock; this wing beat opens the future.

In music and words both, the realized moment annihilates the judgmental self. Artists practice this annihilation. They take themselves apart completely, explode themselves, then reassemble themselves with some fancy design or box or frame—some art—which they then fix and gloss. This is where pure tone really helps, because we can ride it out reliably to the edge of space, over and over again like a shuttle. Tone teaches us annihilation. It makes us disappear so we can reappear one more time according to our contrivances, our words and thoughts and forms. In this going out on tone and coming in on thought, music and words support and complement one another. They are like cousins whose common ancestors have died, who have only each other left, and who confess their love in mazy conversations that go on all night.

Paper Rope

T HE GREATEST DIFFERENCE between music and written words: the difference between air and paper.

All ears that hear can hear music when it is in the air. Music spreads in spherical waves and laps every shore. But the page you now hold no one else is holding. Between you and me these words are a paper rope. We feel the little tugs. You feel me speaking and I feel you reading and listening to me, and then to yourself. Together we are alone, isolated. Right at this moment, no one else is writing what I'm writing. No one but you is reading this line, this very word. These private mysteries circumscribe the two of us in one little boat. You and I. Your eyes and mine. I love your eyes.

3

Sound Self

Central Fish

To KNOW SOUND you have to notice it first. Too bad that civilization requires the knack of folding the senses under, of choosing not to hear. I need to remember how to be a forest animal again, to be the fox who hears everything, or the carp whose shape is the wave of the water itself. I need ways to remind myself that I'm the central fish in this sea of sound.

CLOSING MY EYES

I heard two blind brothers play marimba duets at a restaurant in Bali. They redefined music for me, and what it means to play in the moment. They projected an inner landscape that was so complete that even the diners who didn't get it got it anyway.

When I keep my eyes closed, sound has new meaning. It becomes nourishment, holy food, and my best friend. Lost dimensions are restored: sounds that before had only a surface now have a deep interior. Urgent personal messages are aimed at my head. When I lift open my eyes again the sharp details of these sounds are gone, vaporized in the everyday blaze.

Now, why can't I have the best of both worlds?

HUNTER AND HUNTED

I stand stock-still listening to my surroundings as if I were a hunter, breath shallow, ears connected to stomach. Everything is prey. I consider, in each sound, the advantage.

Now I am the hunted. I hear the threatening edge of each sound, my chances for escape. I gauge distances.

The danger passes. I am the hunter again.

LIKE A BABY

You can wait for the next sound and hear it as if for the first time. Know nothing about the source of the sound—its shape or its purpose. Let it arrive at your ears entirely in the present, with no history. Listen like a new baby listens.

DERVISH LISTENER

Standing with open eyes, I cup my palms behind my ears and slowly turn. This allows me to pinpoint precisely the location of every sound. I become the focus of a sphere, and all the rays are directed toward me. Now dervish mind takes over, and I am motionless at the hub of a spinning world. It is as if I am the sun, and all the light I've been sending out for centuries is coming back.

Be a Movie

A MOVIE IS ABOUT life; it is not life. A movie sound track is not the sound of real life, but rather a sequence of coded signals from cardboard cones, machine lathed, hand polished and set carefully to explode. It has been optimized, equalized, compressed and overlaid, filtered, mixed, and mixed again: "mixed down." It is an art thing, separate and other, and we love to be drawn in, to be willing suckers, to be swept away by sea-foam, lost in violins, petrified by screams. Let this willingness be the basis of a trick:

Be a movie. You're the star. The viewer sees the action through your eyes. This is cinema verité with true-to-life color, never-before-seen verisimilitude. And the sound track is so authentic, so high tech. Okay now: the actual sounds in your life become a *thing*, an object to be examined. By becoming an art object yourself, you position yourself to grasp what you hear *objectively*. Simple. You've already done it a hundred times, buttoned up against the London fog or running in slow motion through blossoming fields. You could try it now, *click*, while you read. Interesting: now we have a movie of a real person reading a book. When you listen to the sound track, all of it, from the nearest sounds of mouth and nose to the middle range of clothing and pages to the distant traffic—

overhead, below, *out there*—you can appreciate the wide range and the artful mix.

For me, the effect of this exercise is invigorating, like scrubbing my face. I realize how profoundly I have been influenced by the sound track all along. Every time I remember to hear this way I am vitalized, but I forget to listen this way. I forget even the promise to remember, and the tricks of memory I myself have invented.

Next time you see a movie or watch a video, notice how the sound track works, how it is contrived to vitalize the images and the action. Then notice how the sound track of the movie you're starring in is similarly contrived. Skillfully done, no?

Advanced movie music: To your life movie add some surreptitious orchestration. The mysterious footsteps outside your door are framed by a somber trombone chord. The man in the mall, carrying one ice cream cone too many, waddles to the sound of a clarinet. And when Devi returns safely from afar, the sound of her car turning into the driveway is overwhelmed by the rush of a full string orchestra with *kettledrums*—muted, but unmistakable.

Ephemerals

THROW THE LAUNDRY into the hamper: be*zooj*. Close the cover: pidge. Take the jacket off the hanger: ke*tang*. Through the open window feel the wind on my face: hong*a*wa. As I move through the world, the world and I make sounds together. But my mind is never quite disengaged from language. Kick those shoes under the bed: ba*joo*puh. I love sound and I love words. Sometimes I love the sound of words even more than the sense they make.

The meanings of most words have become separated from their sounds: concept, territory, potential. Other words seem only to suggest their meanings in their sounds: grope, waddle, push. Onomatopoeic words, whose sounds directly imitate their meanings, are legitimate nouns and verbs: zoom, whiz, buzz, hiss, ding, clank. But there is an additional, frivolous class of words that don't refer to anything beyond their momentary vibrational lives—they are merely mimicry of passing sound, vocal accompaniments rather than proper words. They simply come out of our mouths—they appear in air. These are my specialty. I call them "ephemerals" and I love them most.

I want to feel connected directly in the tongue, in the place where sound and meaning merge without thought. I want to be more alive there than *any*where.

Time to turn the page; listen up: bi*zulip*.

Short Glossary of Ephemerals

az*ah*

chak

chang

gahnk

gahn*jah*bay

gredj

gronk

hazj

hong*a*wah

joop

kej

ke*wang*

*koon*jah

pa*wing*o

puh*jit*

puh*zoo*

r-r-rud*jeh*

tuk*ah, tuk*a

ululul

weef

yoik

zudj

The top of a good list of ephemerals should disappear before you reach the bottom.

Yawning Confession

THE FALSETTO VOICE does not come easily to everyone. But when you yawn, the falsetto kicks in naturally and, for about three seconds in midgape, you can be (if male) the countertenor or (if female) the coloratura of your choice. The smallest muscles of the larynx, when thus maximally stretched, produce a tone reminiscent of a child's, but with an adult's emotion blended in.

I can't remember when I started singing falsetto melodies during yawns, but by now it's a habit that I enjoy in private. I seem to invent favorite arias that come and go in two- or three-month cycles, kind of a yawning hit parade that plays through me. A tune might be Number 1 for weeks, then disappear in a day. Last month I recognized some Hindemith. Most people have personal renditions of their own, often scarcely noticed. I say: notice your yawning songs in all their innocence and their earthiness and quirkiness.

There is so much more to confess! Whole-body stretching songs combine chirps and groans. Sneezes are unique; you can probably recognize each member of your family by his or her very own. Likewise whistles, which we use as personal codes for man and beast—also as a counter-irritant to thought. And what about the sounds some of us make bending over to pick things up? Not to mention those made in regaining our previous dignity?

Permit me here, please, the embarrassment of admitting the difficulty of refraining from forming funny-sounding words when I belch in public. This is what we do when we are seven and our parents are at the movies. But I *am* seven, because that's when I can listen without shame.

And let us consider calmly our repertoire of sighs.

Tell me again why I should listen to such things—things I ordinarily would not hear?

Because they are part of my nature, and my nature is where I begin to learn to listen to the harmony of the world. Even in the most unlikely places, like my body. Especially there.

Sound Apples

THE TWO GIRLS and two boys in my first-grade reading group take turns reading aloud from a book Miss Harlan has chosen. The boy opposite me reads about Janet and Bobby Jones going on a picnic with their parents. The girl next to me reads about the apple orchard near the picnic ground. Now it is my turn.

> "May we pick some apples, Mother?" asked Bobby.
> "Certainly," said Mrs. Jones. "Be sure to pick ripe, sound apples."

I thought I knew the word *sound,* but it doesn't make sense here. Sound is a thing, like thunder, not a way things are, like red. "It says 'sound apples.' What does that mean?" I ask the group. "It *says* 'sound apples,' " one of the girls replies. "Maybe it doesn't," I say, thinking there's a trick. "Well, why don't you go *ask,*" she says.

With my index finger pressed under the word, I carry the book to Miss Harlan, who, busy with the slow group, looks down and says "sound" loudly, as if her best boy were deaf.

Threading my way back to my group, I figure out the

trick: When you tap a good apple with your finger, it makes a big hollow thump that means "I'm delicious and good for you." I want to tell my friends, but by now they are on the next page, and the incident slips into slumber for fifty years, until last week, when I hear myself saying to a student, "The resonance of singing makes your body like a good, sound apple," and the old bright memory comes flooding in.

౿

Sound is a homonym. One root is the Latin *sonare*, "to make noise." The other is thought to be the Greek *iano*, "I heal." So, in English, the meaning can be "audible vibration" or "whole, sane." It is both a noun and an adjective, with complementary connotations. I intend the term "sound self" to cut both ways, to equate conscious hearing with health. Good sound is sane-making. Good vibrations and whole minds are helpmates, exchanging positive energy with each other in brigades that connect their natures.

"What lovely apples," said Mrs. Jones. "Let's each have one for dessert."

Sound Memory

SOUND SPARKS MEMORY. Here are some stories I've remembered thanks to their sounds.

છ

One dreary afternoon in my fourth year, when I was sick and weak, Grandma Clara, wanting to cheer me, reached to the top of the credenza and took down a forbidden object: the sterling silver dinner bell. She said I could ring it all I wanted "whenever you like." Then she left me alone in my room. When I held the bell up to my ear and rang it quietly it sounded exactly like the thin, gleaming roundness it was made of. This bell had always been ceremonial and mute, meant for calling servants who didn't exist. But thanks to my condition, permission had arrived. The forbidden sound was airborne, and I would be safe and whole forever. I wanted the sound to stay soft and private, and be so close to my ear that it would last forever. Ringing the bell again and again put me in a bright swoon. No one said no.

છ

During the summer of that same year I would lie awake on humid nights listening to the crickets and cicadas mixed in

with the sound of my father's typewriter—a lumbering Wood-
stock that added a masculine fusillade to the impersonal
scratchings and scrapings of the insects. I couldn't do anything
about either sound, and the combination made me mad. I felt
invaded by shrillness. But the cross-species rhythms were also
hypnotic and would draw me down eventually into shallow,
noisy sleep.

❧

My morning walk to grade school cut through a secluded
meadow from which I could hear children playing in the distant schoolyard. Filtered through the leaves of many trees,
their whoops and shrieks were softened and fused into a con-
glomerate child, my collective playmate yonder. I remember
thinking, "That's me over there, but I'm standing here. Soon
I'll be over there, *in that part of me.*"

❧

Sound not only informs us but also forms us. When a sound
from long ago remains vibrant, there is a reason. Why has this
sound, of all sounds, stayed alive? Maybe the answer will initiate the writing of a paragraph, a page, or a poem. In writing
this chapter, I made the connection between the sound of a
silver bell and love. I recently bought an extraordinary pair
of Tibetan cymbals whose sound fills me with white delight
"whenever I like." And as I was writing the following poem I
found out that typewriters don't have to mean rejection.

> *Cicadas mating in the astral. Father*
> *typing in the dining room, each letter*
> *a white hit. "I can't sleep."*

"Go back to bed, Bill, I'm earning
your dinner." Today I write in longhand,
gliding back through the dark auroras.
We ate well at our table—roast meats,
fresh fruits. I did sleep, finally.

એ

A variation on this writing practice is to find a friend to trade with. Tell each other the stories of the sounds that changed your lives. Once you start telling and writing sound stories, they keep coming. You can hardly resist retelling them. Why? Because sound wants to keep going. Every sound is like the First Word, a creation story in itself. Sound is the audible form of vital energy that passes through your life. That vitality becomes experience, and then memory, and then your pen writing or your tongue talking, and then people reading and hearing and being moved to tell their own stories.

Name History

A NCIENT WISDOM SAYS that to name a thing is to call forth its being. In the beginning was the word; not long after *my* beginning, my parents named me Bill. Plain, but safe. Thirty-three years later, my Sufi teacher named me Alla-uddin. *Alla* sounds like a name for God; *uddin* means "on the path." Alla-uddin could mean "seeker" or "teacher." When I first heard him pronounce the new name it had a strange light in it; it rang a bell. But when I saw it written I drew back. I thought it looked foreign and wore a funny hat.

My Sufi friends started to call me by my new name with a sort of pointed piousness. They Americanized the original Arabic pronunciation *ah LA 'uh DEEN* (the middle syllable, *'uh,* starting with a glottal stop in the throat; the final vowel somewhere between *een* and *in*) into *allOW-dean* (the end of the *OW* diphthong slightly drawn out toward the *oooh* sound). It began to take on a midwestern twang. I began to like it. It was musical, with a nice four-syllable float to it: *de BIB de dop.* Unlike Bill. I dropped the hyphen and one of the *d*s and told people that it sounds like the two English words *allow* and *dean,* and it caught on.

Not with my oldest friends, though. Former high school classmates in Cincinnati tolerantly overlooked Bill's other name. Chicagoans, who have a healthy mistrust of imported spirituality, began to call me Billy.

When I made a solo piano album for Windham Hill in 1987—my first (and last) hope for the mass marketing of my music—I felt the name Allaudin would mean professional death. Written on the page, it looks impossible to pronounce, especially in the company of Mathieu, which for generations has been Americanized from the French *maht YEU* into *MATH yew.* I thought of becoming Matt Williams or Al Matthews. I finally decided to hide behind W. A. Mathieu. When I told this to Windham Hill producer Will Ackerman, he said, "Sounds literary." That settled it.

So my friends call me allOW-dean, my mamma calls me Bill, some call me "WA"; others call me Uncle Al. I am partial to Dr. Overtone and especially—since I am a Sufi sheikh (pronounced *shake*)—Sheikh Allegro, which seems to me to have the appropriate tone.

Recalling name history is not equally easy for everyone because the sound of what people call us, or used to call us, is a deep mirror that carries the past along with it. But if I listen to the mere sound of my name—reducing it to a stream of innocent phonemes—I just might be able to hear it fresh in the present. If I'm not wild about Bill, it is after all not the fault of the soft and pleasant *B,* or the *i,* full of afternoon light, darkening to a mysterious *uh* as it approaches the mellifluous *ll.* And one cannot help but notice the lovely, lilting *ll* itself, half lift, half lullaby.

But historical associations do build up, and they can overpower the intrinsic sound of any name. Then maybe it's time to find a new one. You have every right to be called what you want to be called. A person's name is his or hers to change. Most folks are self-conscious about changing their names, naturally, but friends and co-workers are often quicker to get used to your new name than you are. There's no harm in asking, incidentally, "What's my secret name?" The secret name of Jules Feiffer's cartoon character Bernard is Spike.

Sensitivity to my own name makes me sensitive to how I address others. It feels right to spin good energy toward a person on the sound of his name, or her name. That sound might still be spinning a thousand years from now.

Voice Mask

I TAPE-RECORD my lessons with the North Indian singer Pandit Pran Nath. He sings a phrase. I repeat it. He sings, I repeat. The idea is to sound like him. I take the tape home and study it during the week. I so love the gentle sweetness of his voice. But when I listen to my responses on the tape, I say to myself, "Oh, shut up." This has gone on for twenty years.

One day recently I asked myself, "What is it exactly that you don't like about your voice?" The answer, long avoided, was: "My voice is harsh and pushy. Always over the edge, always proving something. When it *is* soft and accommodating, it is lying."

Having said this much, I was able to continue: "Okay. Everything I hear in my voice is true. But it is still, after all, my own voice, as much a part of my maturity as it is a part of my immaturity. So why not do whatever I can to refine it toward my ideal voice?" With this new resolve, I found I could identify the qualities I didn't like in my voice during the actual moment of speaking or singing, and that gave me the opportunity to row gentler waters, to soften the moment. Then, at last Sunday's lesson, after one of my musical responses, my teacher said sincerely, "You have a beautiful voice" (which he pronounces *wo-ees*).

I did not turn into an exotic bird on the spot. But I have

been feeling encouraged, since then, to seek what is attractive in my voice. The compliment, still ringing in my ears, gives me leverage. My teacher was not just being nice. His own beauty let him hear the beauty in another, and he said what he heard. That really, really helped me.

જ

At one time or another practically everyone is put off by the sound of his or her voice. Too wimpy or rough; too fawning or eager; or just plain ugly. The hardest blow is to suddenly discover the voices of your parents coming out of your own mouth.

> *"I stood in the doorway yelling down at my daughter and what I heard was my own mother."*

> *"I was trying to get out of the loan deal and I heard the voice of good old unreliable Dad, weaseling out of taking me to the game."*

Most of us need independence from our parents, especially same-gender parents. It's a tricky predicament to unexpectedly hear their persona folded into your own. Just as problematic: witnessing your childhood voice involuntarily return in the presence of your parents. This happens to adult children in their sixties as well as in their twenties.

જ

Persona comes from the Greek word for "mask." It refers to the face we use to meet the world. The sound of my persona *is* my voice. When my inner and outer worlds are out of balance my voice reflects that. The more I try to cover the imbalance, the more the mask grins and grimaces in distortions I can scarcely see or hear.

But if you actually listen to the sound of your voice instead of closing your ears to it, it can reveal your persona to you in a helpful way. Don't try to change it. If your voice sounds insincere, don't try to make it sound sincere. Let your effort go into *being* sincere. Your voice reflects your truest feeling. Work on the feeling, not the reflection. As your feeling comes into balance, so will your voice. The voice is a faithful ally in the work of refining feeling. It can tell you when to give a little slack, and when to be strict with yourself. Word by word, phrase by phrase, if you are listening it will lead you toward balance.

It is a wonderful thing to hear the beauty in another's voice and let that person know it. When you hear the depth or longing in your friend's voice as something true and good, point that out, be a kind mirror. You are not only helping her, you are helping yourself hear your own voice in a positive light. That goodness you hear in your friend's voice is in yours also.

Inner Voice

I TALK TO MYSELF NONSTOP. When I read, my inner voice is like light flickering behind closed eyelids. When I speak it is like a backstage mama hidden by curtains, pointing and nodding. It doesn't need grammar or syntax, or even words, but uses a prelanguage of judgmental surges—flavors of yes, no, and maybe. It can coo like a dove or cry like a baby, or come unglued, chattering like a monkey. This inner sound has its own quality and cadence, and is distinct from my speaking voice. It is a language meant for the internal ear only and knows no other way to be. While my outer voice is saying, "No, I don't remember what I wore to Alice's wedding," my inner voice is infused with feelings and textures from Alice's wedding in a language that would vaporize in air.

I feel the voices of my bright and dark selves as if I were actually hearing them, but perhaps it is metaphysical to refer to them as sound; maybe it is more clear to say that pre-sound unfolds by immeasurable degrees into spoken language. When I pay attention to my pre-voice I can feel the littlest muscles of my tongue and larynx move, or get set to move. When my thoughts are calm, damped down to perception without comment, then these muscles quiet down too, and my internal sound becomes murmurous, like bottom water undulating in smooth waves. My breath slows. Then suddenly the phone rings and the voice pipes up like a parrot, "Now who's that?"

The mind that knows how to produce this inner voice also knows how to calm it. All of the many meditative methods for modulating the inner voice begin with the desire to hear it. The clearer the desire, the clearer the hearing. At the core of the cooing and the chattering is always a more purposeful voice, a more harmonious sound. And at the center of that sound, like a motionless place in the current, is plain old being-as-it-is, which means self-acceptance and the peace that grows around that like a blue pond.

Breathing Sound

I F YOU LISTEN to the sound of your breathing as you read this, you can hear the difference between a breath through your nose and one through your mouth. You can notice the high clicks as your tongue moves around, and as you swallow.

All streaming air sounds somewhat similar, like escaping steam or river rapids—white noise. But there are shades of white. Air currents whooshing through tunnels and whistling around corners audibly take on the characteristics of the terrain they pass through. Air through the nose sounds different from air through the mouth. An in-breath sounds different from an out-breath. These sounds reflect the inner topography of the body.

Try this: say *sh-h-h-h* as though you were asking someone to quiet down. While you do that, purse your lips forward, as if saying *uuu*, and move them slowly back to form *eeee*. The general area of pitch seems to rise and fall—variations on air. Are there identifiable pitches? Not usually; more like large fuzzy areas of high-pitched sound.

Everyone has a private flute sound. Make an extremely gentle hissing sound, ever so softly, while bringing your tongue as far forward toward your teeth as you can. It is a very quiet whistle. Now slowly move it back, then forward again.

The whistle makes a song. A little tongue/hard palate music: "Wind Inside."

These little wind songs are present in your breathing sound, but so sweet and hidden that you have to scan for them. When you are listening with enough clarity, the sounds of ordinary breathing become a new way of being inside yourself, another dimension of your oldest friend.

Notice also the shallowness or heaviness of your breath cycle. How long is the pause at the bottom of the breath? How long at the top? There is a fine saying in Paul Reps's *Zen Flesh, Zen Bones:* ". . . as the breath curves up to down—realize."

Ultimate Mixer

I AM CLEANING UP the dishes after lunch for two, carrying food and tableware back into the kitchen. Devi has just turned on the dishwasher full of last night's dishes. It clicks into its wash cycle, making the grinding, whooshing noise I love to hate. On the dining room table the portable radio is still tuned to Giants baseball—we've been listening to the game, laughing and groaning over our sandwiches. Now, midway between kitchen and dining room, I notice how the crowd noise from the game mixes evenly with the whoosh of the dishwasher so that at a certain point the inclination of my head an inch forward or backward tilts the balance from a washing crowd to a cheering dishwasher. Pickle jar in one hand, mayonnaise in the other, I stand transfixed at the cusp, gently rocking back and forth, barely rotating my head, savoring the tiny arc between crowd and machine.

෨

Suspended above the bedroom door is a wooden Balinese buffalo bell. Its clapper is a bunch of three-inch porcupine quills. The twiggy dry sound is scarcely louder than the wind in the Balinese rice, but it brings to memory a time of exquisite calm; a touch does it. Favorite bells and chimes are strung elsewhere in our house and yard from rafters and tree limbs, an allowance of high vibes I've learned to treasure.

ⱷ

Noticing your soundscape is the first thing. Then you tinker with it continuously until you and it learn to coevolve. Like a recording engineer who mixes alternative versions of a piece into an optimal version, you are the ultimate mixer of what you hear. I've learned only gradually to take responsibility for the sounds of my life, inside and outside both. I realize how I form them and they form me. I don't think we have to make do with what merely chances by. In fact, we are sitting at the controls, guiding and being guided by the vibrational current we are both in and of.

4

The Music Mirror

Some Music Mirrors

I'VE BEEN THINKING about the reciprocity of music, how it is one of the many mirrors in the universe of mirrors we belong to. When music comes into me from the outside, it seems like I am looking at a huge projection of myself. When music goes out of me from my inside, I feel like I am giving back, in my fashion, a picture of the world. These reflections all reflect one another; to listen to music is to blur the distinction between inside and outside.

This could be a threatening situation (whose food is this? whose air? whose nation?), and my response could be warlike. But the plane of the music mirror is a boundary we love to play in, not fight over. Somehow we feel more alive and connected when we are looking into and out of these glasses we construct. There is a surge of understanding between us, and some long deep gaze into what we might become.

No one knows how it works, of course, so let the following observations and descriptions be only a way we have of talking about ourselves.

SYMPHONY ORCHESTRA

An orchestra is playing a lively piece by Bach and all the players are up and out of their chairs. Smoothly bowing their violins and crisply tonguing their French horns, they are walking lively in the streets of their towns and moving comfortably in the rooms of their houses. While eating, laughing, and attending meetings, everyone is playing an instrument and never missing a beat of Bach. Each person's part is well played, each melodic line a life story, yet the ensemble soars and dives in a single woven work. When it is over everyone goes to sleep for a few minutes wherever they are. Then everyone wakes up and a new piece begins, and again, every note is in place. The stores and banks busy as hives, the players sawing and tooting—all are harnessed by the music to a common good, an idealized life of individual integrity and communal weal.

The gorgeous polyphony of symphonic music can evoke such images of the social ideal. A well-turned-out suite by Handel is a metaphor of harmonious humanity. While we are sitting in the concert hall motionless and absorbed, the little village of musicians onstage is realizing a utopia. This is what life could be if it were music.

Now let's reenact our scenario differently. We and our friends are going about daily business in the usual way: running errands, sitting at desks, cooking, sharing confidences over coffee, waiting in line. Now add in the musical instruments, but this time not the actual physical instruments, only the sounds they produce. Imagine that everyone's work and play and thought externalizes spontaneously as the sound of an instrument; one person is a clarinet, another a drum. There is no single composer—the composition is collective. Each plays a crucial part in the creation of an entire symphony that all are listening to. Everyone clearly hears everyone else, and all together the ensemble feels enormous and exhilarating. What would be the sound of that music?

POLYPHONY

At the core of the legacy of European classical music is the technique called *polyphony*. Here is my definition of polyphony: You sing a song, a good song that sounds fine all by itself. I sing a song that sounds just as fine all by itself. Yet when we sing together, something happens: the two songs, while distinctly retaining their original characters, sound better together than separately. The union is more satisfying than the separation. The two songs might, incidentally, be quite different from one another, or they might be similar. They could, in fact, be identical but begin at different moments, as in a round. In any case, the contrapuntal tenet is that individual integrity finds its transcendence in collective expression. This technique, perfected in the sixteenth century and practiced with increasing rarity today, is, in its simplest form, as accessible to each of us as "Row, Row, Row Your Boat."

Imagine yourself and your most intimate friend in a deep conversation, feeling one another's feelings while talking soul talk. Effortlessly your speech turns into music: two braided instruments, a clarinet and a cello, or a French horn and trombone, or two alto flutes, or a soprano saxophone and an electric bass. What would *that* sound be?

OPERA

Operatic drama, extravagant as it often is, nevertheless lives tenaciously from generation to generation, and appears in culture after culture. We love to see ourselves proscenium-boxed and choreographed-sculpted as singing gods, hurling forth our deepest secrets in magnificent arias, while the assembled bands and choruses approve, condemn, and egg us on. What if you opened your eyes only to discover that you and your friends were onstage in an opera, midscene? There are no special costumes or sets. The scenery is what you see now, the costumes what you are wearing now. There is no score: the music consists of the sounds you are hearing now.

ALONE/TOGETHER: CHOIR SINGING

Most everyone has sung in a choir, if only the "Happy Birthday" choir. When singing with others, you can feel the whole group in your tissues. The harmonies are so palpable, the togetherness so uplifting, that social and spiritual ideals are sparked into real time. We discover ourselves inhaling and exhaling within the same harmonious nature—humanity organized by sound.

But there is a condition for choir singing: in order to sing *tutti*—with everyone—you have to know your part *solo*—alone. You can't be a member of the collective until you can function individually.

In a choir, the boundary between self and others is not an intellectual consideration, it is a matter of moment-to-moment discrimination. You deal with it—consciously or not—with every breath. If you lose the shape of your musical line you are suddenly an outsider, perhaps a threat. At the same time, the ongoing resonance helps you find your way. You are continuously adjusting the boundaries between where the self ends and the rest of the world begins. The boundaries shrink and fade and leap; you cross and recross them in a greatly serious sort of play.

PIANO CONCERTO

The dynamic between self and other is most starkly revealed in a good classical piano concerto. A piano is special in the way it is itself a little orchestra. A pianist's fingers can seem to cover the entire keyboard, often giving the effect of several players. Yet as listeners, we know—because we've been told, or because we see with our own eyes—that one person is playing all those notes. Hence, the piano soloist becomes a model of self-reliance, of resourceful individualism. An orchestra, in contrast, is an ideally harmonious society. In a piano concerto these two perceptions—the omnipotent protagonist and the monolithic aggregate—are played off against one another in a relationship that is in turn caressing or competitive, flirtatious or contentious. Yet always the polarity of the individual against the many is preserved, drawing us into the action.

What is amazing is the overall unity of the piece. As the drama of self and society plays itself out, we, safe in our seats, are witnessing an entire life span. The music is giving us a picture of our paradoxical selves once again—a good long look.

What would your life sound like if it were a piano concerto? Not the whole *thing*, just a few choice segments. Would there be many moods? An overall sweetness or struggle?

Would there be clamorous rackets? Stuck places?

Roaring and soaring?

Simple Is Complex

THE SAME TEACHER who taught me jazz—Buddy Hiles—
was the first person in my life to zero in on my intellectual masking. Even when I was thirteen and knew hardly any
music theory, I wanted to know all the answers to all the puzzles. "Show me some more complicated chords," I'd ask, but
Buddy knew I needed to see the opposite face. One day we
were sitting at the piano writing down chords for saxophones
when he took my pencil away and said, "Listen to this."

Then he started to whistle "Old Man River" very beautifully and very loudly. I was vexed at first—my puzzles had
been interrupted and my racing mind flagged down. I had
never heard such a loud whistle and I had never looked at a
man's face up close for a long, open time. Buddy was thirty-
three years old, brown-black, with a wide, beautiful flat nose,
generous lips, and thirty extra pounds on him. He was a cool
operator but he was kind and compassionate, and he showed
me human closeness. Now I was staring at the little beads of
sweat along his fuzzy upper lip, at the stubble under his lower
lip, and the puckered hole between them, which was producing a sonic knife of joy. Joy for the wisdom of old rivers, their
endurance, his endurance, his life, his teaching of the staring
white boy. So much bright air from such a quivering, tiny,
dark space. My ears were splitting and my heart, my young

heart that craved to love beyond its adolescence, was opened. Then, still whistling, his gaze locked into mine; my eyes went wide. He stopped and grinned a cocky grin. "Jes' keeps rollin'," he said and chuckled from his belly, because he knew that I had heard his air streaming back to an ancient time.

Twenty years later, in San Francisco, I was learning a kind of devotional circle dancing from Sufi Sam Lewis. But I didn't want to be just another dancer in the circle, I wanted to be in the center along with the mysterious guitarists and the fascinating drummers. One day I spied a tambourine and, gingerly at first, added a bright metallic etching to the deep *dooms* and high *beks* of the goatskin dumbeks and the strums and twangs of the guitars and the full throats of the singers.

Now I have been playing tambourine at the center of Sufi dancing for twenty-five years, walking slowly around the inside of the circle against the current of the dancers. What I love is the astringent simplicity of the instrument. It is not a keyboard; it is not a cello. Rattling metal disks is what it is. The trick in tambourine playing is to lay each little rippling vibration into the whole of the music so as to outline and define the rhythms, just as the outlines of a drawing define the figures. One scarcely notices outlines—they are the membranes of the cell, holding and shaping the life inside. The shaping requires, for the tambourine player, total concentration. If the strokes are too bold or controlling, they will stifle the life. If they are careless they will unbalance and topple it. The great lesson is to learn to shake with the right force at the right time, and to be generous and whole in that. No chords, no cadenzas or polyphonic invention, just perfect taps and shakes. The more you enter into these simple gestures the more meaning they take on, the more complete they become and the more you are completed in them. Their little silver cymbals just keep rolling along.

Home

THE PATTERN THE SUN CASTS setting through the leaves of these maples is no different here in southern Ohio than across the river in northern Kentucky, or down in Missouri or over in Virginia. There is no magic magnet under the black soil. What is pulling me, then? Why is my chest so warm? Because I have returned to the woods near my boyhood home, a woods that, after fifty years, still recognizes me by name.

It seems like wherever we are isn't half so important as how far from home we are, and how long we've been away, and how difficult it will be to get back. And when we are home we reckon by how long it will be till we leave again.

Home is a condition of human life. Even if we are nomads, we have a home *some*where. What rare being seeks to be homeless? As I define my home it defines me. How else to explain the love I feel for the newly painted trim on our old white farmhouse? I mixed the color myself: Smiling Blue.

∾

We have developed a homing instinct for musical pitch. The ear's ability to remember a given pitch, and return to it at will, defines the life of a piece of music like the homing instinct defines real life.

When I remember a given musical pitch, what is it exactly that I'm remembering?

Let's say I am reading a book. I sing a tone. I go on reading. I sing it again and read some more. I sing it again, think a little bit, read, follow some mindful meander, sing it again. It is intriguing how the tone I sing can be pitched the same each time, even with these interruptions. You have the ability to remember pitch even if you think you don't, or have been told you don't. Some people have developed it more than others, but everyone has it to some degree. It might take a little practice to find it, and a little courage perhaps, but it is as naturally a part of your portion as is your capacity to discern whether a line is straight or crooked.

Here is an extension of the practice. I sing a tone. Then I sing it again, but internally, without making a sound. Then I sing it outside again, then again inside.

What is happening here? A specific frequency is being recalled with extraordinary exactness. How can it be that we bid the fibers of our larynx muscles to vibrate, say, 220 times per second, then hear that vibration internally (what is vibrating?) and then again, by command, externalize the vibration? Who is telling what to whom? I wish I knew.

I wish I knew something else: How can a tone be a *place*? How can a pattern in air be a home we can leave and return to? Yet, entrenched somewhere between your ears is the *territory* of music, sensible and concrete as the woods of home. Even more strange: every piece of classical music you've ever heard that's in a key—like Mozart's Symphony No. 41 in C Major, or Chopin's Piano Concerto No. 1 in E Minor, or Bach's Magnificat in D Major—begins by establishing, usually from note one, the generating tone of the entire piece. A symphony in D starts in D, immediately telling you "D is home." With no trouble, every listener from the trained to the nonlit-

erate knows (and *remembers*) that D is home. Not every listener would think to say that, or be able to sing D if asked to
sing the home note. But every attentive listener feels a sense of
completion when the music, after many journeys to the foreign climes of other keys, finally does return, older and more
experienced, to D. That is the odd part: even people without
an especially developed sense of pitch feel this effect of return-
ing home. You receive meaning from the home pitch just as
you know, without knowing you know, how far from your
house you are. Your sense of home is always changing but it
is always there, in music as in life.

In music, journeys away from home can be described in
terms of both how far and how long. Take the example of a
trill, which starts on a note, then goes to the note just above
it, then goes back to the original. This musical move, though
uncomplicated, can nonetheless be magical. What if you make
the higher note much longer than the lower one? Much, much
longer? The plot thickens. What if you alternate rapid trills
and stately trills, or speed them up and slow them down gradually? You could contrast the dynamics, also the timbres. Each
new way the second note relates to the first note is a new way
of being away, a new twist to the story. What if the higher
note becomes a home away from home? Could you reestablish
the original sense of home?

Music that has a "key note," a home note, is called tonal
music. Most of the music in the world is tonal; it generates its
meaning, as it proceeds, from the relationship of its many
notes to the key note. Tonal journeys are sometimes labyrin-
thine and sophisticated or, in visceral episodes, highly dra-
matic. Sometimes they are playful; sometimes we get lost for
ages, then reemerge battered, with our memories hanging by
a thread. In the music of this century we can end up somewhere else from where we began—in another key—yet we still

qualify the *else*ness by how far away we end up from the original key. Our hunger for and delight in tonality is the very spine of music, the central beam that holds up the house of sound.

Buddy Hiles, by way of introducing me to composition, told me, "It doesn't matter how far you go out, it only matters how you get back." We are not so concerned with how Lassie, a thousand miles from home, got where she is now, but how she finds her way back again. Meaning and value derive from the transformational effect of the long journey.

The search for home in music is not passive but active, desperate and grasping. Music does what any passionate protagonist would do: it probes any alley and pursues any promise to get what it wants. The force in us that seeks to complete the life cycle is at the core of musical form. To travel musically is to continually harken back to your origins.

Try listening to some music from India or some Scottish bagpipe music or any music made over a drone. If you concentrate on the drone as you listen to the melody, you can witness, tone by tone, how your feelings are affected. Every least ripple of music desires the drone, lies in wait for it, avoids it, flirts and dances with it, and finally reunites with it.

It's the same when you listen to Haydn or Mozart. But in European classical music, the drone is not sounding in the air all the time, it is sounding in your memory. A home away from home is set up by moving to a different key, and a home away from *it*, like tenting up slope from your vacation cabin. There are false sanctuaries, temporary keeps, and beguiling wayhouses before we eventually come home to die wise and satisfied so we can be born again in the next piece.

Memory Bin

SOMETIMES YOU NEED *two* mirrors to look at something—
like the back of your head. We have been referring to
music as a kind of mirror; let's for the moment use another
kind of mirror: words. We are used to language; it seems right
at home on the tongue, a part of us. Maybe it will help us see
around corners.

Consider, as you read this sentence, an aspect of the reading process—not *any* aspect, but a particular one—that we
ordinarily take for granted: the way in which we store up, in a
kind of a loose net, or gelatinous bin (gelatin reminds me of
something that I'll mention later if I remember, which is unlikely) the information that has so far accrued—including in-
terpolations (there are, for example, a total of 522 letters and
three numerals in this sentence)—but has not yet coalesced
into its full, all-embracing, comprehensive, inclusive (I am
using, of course, *Roget's Thesaurus*, Fifth Edition, newly published by HarperCollins), panoramic sweep of meaning. Did
we make it through? Notice, when reading, how your inner
voice is scanning and scavenging for the logic, how it rises
silently as it holds the tension, and then relaxes into cadential
valleys. Toward the end of a long sentence, even as the eyes
are seeking the first word of the next one, the sequestered
phrases and dangling images are sucked rushing into proper

configuration. The word bin empties, then fills and empties again; like a bellows, it fans the light of meaning.

When words are held in the bin, part of their meaning is in limbo. The identity of puns, misunderstood words, or words whose definitions are unknown, is held up for questioning, indefinitely detained at customs. But then, in a good sentence, the bin empties with a final whoosh of pleasure. Short sentences refresh the bin. Reiterative sentences regenerate its holding power and reassure the reader.

The word bin does something peculiar with present time: it expands it. The perplexity of the past (words whose meanings have not yet clarified), the immediacy of the present (these words right now), and the potential of the future (various possible meanings that occur to us as we read) are all suspended as equals during the long moment of a sentence. In a way, time can flow backward. The significance of an earlier event can alter as later events clarify; the past can change. It is as though, at a fork in the road, instead of making up our mind which road to take, we take both roads at once, at least for a while, until events tell us which one we are actually on. One might call the expanded present a kind of bifurcation behavior, a way we have of being ambiguous, as if that would momentarily widen our vision or lengthen our reach. Language presents this behavior in a form we can examine anytime we want to.

Every speaker or writer builds into her use of language an assumed attention span, a memory norm. The short sentences of journalism and the rapid-fire cadences of radio and television (especially the commercials) belie the anticipated ability, on the part of the consumer, to remember words. At the other extreme, some academic writing uses unnecessarily long sentences as if to fend off the reader whose mental retention does not meet certain criteria. Proust and Faulkner lay monstrous sentences upon the mind; Hemingway found a charismatic use of short ones. Annie Dillard writes looping, balletic sentences that land the reader effortlessly on point, balanced and ready for more. Good writing naturally increases the capacity of the memory bin. But whatever the style or the purpose of the writer or speaker, there is the unspoken but real assumption that the short-term memory of the reader or listener has a certain minimal capacity.

When you become aware of how language uses memory in an expanded present, the act of listening to music can take on new interest. Of course, some music is not really meant to be understood so much as felt or danced to. The phrases of pop and dance music are purposefully short and reiterative in the extreme; this is also the path of trance. Music to dream by has long spacious phrases that move slowly. There is not much in it *to* remember—which doesn't discredit it. We need to dance and we need to dream. We also need to meet our minds. Music composed for listening's sake is a house of mirrors wherein you recognize your own intelligence.

A phrase of music is much like a sentence. A complete theme—a group of musical phrases—is like a paragraph. A discrete segment of a piece made up of a coherent group of themes and their connecting links—like the exposition of a sonata movement—resembles a chapter. An entire movement of a piece is like a section of a book. The piece is the book. Do we remember everything in a book? More or less, depending on the book. Do we remember everything in a piece? Sure, if we want to.

One problem with trying to remember is the fear of forgetting. I, for instance, have introphobia. When it comes time to introduce my wife, my parents, my children, or even (sometimes especially) myself to anybody else, my palms sweat and my tongue freezes. God forbid I should be required to introduce two mere acquaintances to one another. To stave off panic I rehearse; I practice faultless stratagems. But even when I succeed I'm a wreck. I think a similar problem exists for many people when they want to listen to—and actually hear—intelligent music. There is the fear of not being able to remember, or even recognize, what is heard.

Here is technique I use to face that fear of forgetting. You pick a piece of concert music (i.e., music composed to be listened to), any piece you like or *could* like. You find a timepiece that tells the seconds. Then you play the music, and time how long it goes on before it changes. Change means anything you perceive it to mean; different listeners will have different perceptions. The idea is to find out what change means to you and track it. Any definition of change will do as long as you are listening. Jot down the number of seconds elapsed before the next change: this may range from two seconds to forty-five seconds, or longer. You are tracking musical clauses, perhaps sentences, perhaps paragraphs. Your list of numbers may hint at the hidden assumption the composer made about the listener's memory bin. The exercise gets you to concentrate on what the music is saying.

You can expand your musical memory bin by doing an exercise I call "*AA BB CC.*" Sing or play a simple phrase made up of a few notes only—as few as two notes, and no more than you can easily remember. Then repeat that phrase precisely. (We can represent the phrase as *A*; with its repeat it becomes *AA*.) Next sing a completely different phrase, keeping it simple and well within the range of your short-term memory. Now repeat *that* phrase exactly. (That was *BB*.) Now a new phrase with its exact repeat (*CC*). We have invented the form *AA BB CC DD EE* . . . , in which you function as your own echo.

This form generates a musical texture that can be attractive in itself. But beyond that, it requires you to listen carefully enough to your phrases to reiterate them, and that means taking responsibility for each note. Gradually you will be able to recall longer and more intricate phrases; it is astonishing how far back the arm of musical memory can reach. The more developed your musical memory becomes, the more you will recognize it as the prime condition for the intellectual pleasure of music.

Awareness of how music unfolds has sensitized me to the varieties of cogency in daily life: the inner logic of conversations with others and myself, and the spinning out of life's stories within stories. The examination of one's own memory can be scary, but with the light of an eye that sees itself, it's never *too* scary.

Whatsa Matta wid da Bass?

IN 1984 I RETURNED briefly from California to Chicago to play a house concert for a Sufi friend. She lived up on the thirtieth floor of a glass high-rise in an elegant suite with a view of the city. Safe. Posh. My thirty listeners were white, educated, and also safe and posh, like me, or so I thought.

I played a nice concert, as befitted my surroundings: gentle, refined, intricately spun, yes. Afterward I gave a little lecture about my music and asked for questions. "Who were your spiritual teachers?" I answered. "Who are your favorite composers?" I said who. From the corner, a rough alto profundo: "Whatsa matta wid da bass?" Submerged at the end of a downy couch was a dumpy woman with shaggy eyebrows, a pronounced nose, and a dark upper lip.

"Do you mean the bass on the piano"—it was a nice Steinway with a full bass—"or the way I play it?"

More insistent now, stubborn and garrulous, "Whatsa matta wid da bass?"

Oh well, I thought, and launched into a long defensive answer, not realizing how my button had been pushed. I identify strongly, I explained, with Mozart, and it seems to me that Mozart's music is centered just a few notes higher than most other music. Also I like the piano soprano; I *save* the bass for

added effectiveness when I *do* use it. I paused and arched my
eyebrows. "OK?"

"Yeah. But whatsa *matta* wid it?"

People were snickering and I was squirming. "You
wanted to hear more of it, right?"

"Yeah. More."

"Next time," I said cheerily, but I was angry.

The incident stayed with me. A few months later I figured
out my anger: the woman, who was very familiar with and
accepting of her own ways, had sensed me hiding something.
Gruff as she was, she was balanced and honest, and she called
my cards. I realized what a safe, posh concert I had played,
and how I do avoid the bass. In the 1960s and 1970s my music
was full of turmoil and aggression. Lately it had been undergo-
ing a latter-day revision, a spiritualization, a purge. But I had
thrown out the baby with the bath. I was afraid of the deep,
gruff part of me showing. That is why this woman who put
her deep self right out there threatened me so. By speaking
out she made me, eventually, listen to my own music, including the missing bass, which I still have a little trouble with.
But as it turns out, there's absolutely nothing the matter with
it at all.

KNOWING THE BASS

Everyone *feels* the bass; not many people *know* the bass. Here's
an experiment. Find a recording of a piece you like and play
it through once, concentrating on the lowest sounding tones
only—the bass line. Identify with the musicians playing those
tones. You can feel how they are supporting the timbers that
shore up the weight of the world.

"You Can't Do Anything Twice"

M Y DRUMMER FRIEND George Marsh said to me one day, when I asked him to repeat something he had played, "You can't do anything twice." In truth, there are ways in which an action can be repeated and ways in which it cannot.

In 1974 the Sufi Choir was asked to sing on early-morning TV. Our call was for a 6:00 A.M. taping; the show was to be broadcast at 8:00 A.M. Some of us stayed up all night to make the call; others straggled in on a few hours sleep. The program was called "Mystical Experience." I had my doubts.

At 6:45, eighteen glazed singers stood staring into a camera lens. The production assistant clacked the slate board, called out "Mystical Experience, Take One," and gamely we began to sing. A minute into the shot, however, the camera malfunctioned and we had to abort the take. "Take it from the top," called the director. Once again the production assistant clacked the slate board, but this time he said "Mystical Experience, Take Two."

We tried to be professional, but we knew a cosmic joke when we heard one, and we lost our cool, every one of us, and had to sing through our giggles and nudges and rollings of the eyes. In a deeper way, we were embarrassed because we found ourselves in the odd position of quantifying the uncountable and packaging the uncontainable. But it did wake us up, and we sang less like night owls and more nearly like morning larks.

e⋄

Music thrives on certain kinds of repetition. In Bach, for instance, little bits of music are heard again and again in changing contexts. Old events and new surroundings are continuously redefining one another.

Dance music and devotional chanting put us in touch with our physical periodicities: the even strokes of running and swimming, the spasms of orgasm, the nodding of davening, the fidelity of the heart itself, and of the breath. Dancing and chanting can heighten and prolong the normal cycles of the body so as to seem to suspend time.

There is a kind of music, called minimal music, that causes us to examine the nature of repetition itself. It and its composers have taken some critical heat. The works of Steve Reich, John Adams, and Philip Glass are characterized by reiteration of bits of music, sometimes, it seems, beyond the listener's fury. You have to sit on your hands and pay attention to minimal music. It doesn't allow the mental stimulation of new keys and chords as does classical music, or body joy, as does dance music. It means to get you close as possible to doing something—or listening to something being done— twice, and more than twice. When you are close enough you begin to see fully the way in which it cannot be done. It cannot be done because creation is evolving, and you along with it. You can't step into the same river twice because, of course, the river has moved. But employing music as the means for this epiphany is more than some people can bear. They decline to play the moment-to-moment game of self-examination in the concert hall; instead they get bored and rebellious. Not only listeners. Some symphonic musicians so loathe this music, which requires them to play the same bar dozens of times, that they have lobbied their unions to contractually limit its performance by their orchestras.

Yet the perpetrators of minimal music want listeners and players to break through the boredom and allow a new awareness wherein the more things stay the same the more they change. This new kind of change, which can be enlightening, then becomes the substance of the music.

The question of repetition opens up a wider question about nature: the relation of pattern to chaos. It is true that every time we pin something down, inside that hard edge of certainty is a kite in the wind. Inside pattern: chaos; inside chaos: pattern, spiraling inward, finally, to your own perceptions. You meet yourself. The observer and the observed are the same. You are what you are hearing.

I have often had this experience while listening to music, and I think many others have also. I want to bring that experience forward—it is my reason for writing. Each time it happens to me I think I've invented a new way of saying what happened, but then I think, How could it ever be said properly?

๛

If you repeat some easy thing many times, like tapping on the table, while observing what is going on inside of you, including your resistance, you may have trouble concentrating, but that's the point: it is hard enough to do anything once, let alone twice. Indeed, the most difficult thing is to do something completely one time. If your action is complete, it is unique; you never need to count higher than one; you never need to be bored, ever, ever.

Consonance and Dissonance
(No! No! No!)

I N CHICAGO, in the 1960s, I am hard at work studying the
scores of contemporary composers, Karlheinz Stockhausen
among them. He is fashionable; besides, I am interested in the
rhythmic problems of his piano pieces. When I hear that
David Tudor, one of the best new-music pianists, is playing a
concert—including Stockhausen—in my neighborhood, I
make sure to be there.

Nice hall. Three hundred intellectually aware Chicago
liberals with "we recognize the music of the future" written
on their foreheads. Clubby, knowing atmosphere. I sit near
the back, on the center aisle, and soak it up. David Tudor
comes out and starts to do Stockhausen just fine. We all enjoy
this brainy, unrelieved dissonance that flirts so sagely with
chaos. But the smugness is broken by a commotion in the
third row.

At first a muffled sobbing, then a woman's distressed
voice crying, "No!" We crane and whisper; the music, unper-
turbed, plays on in noisy fits and starts. More *no*s, wild this
time, and insistent. *A claque,* I think. *A rude demonstration
against our music.* Then a genuine disruption as the woman is
led up the center aisle by a man on either side; a bride in

reverse, I think. The men are trying to be gentle and reassuring. They speak quietly to her. "No, no, no, no!" she yells as she is ushered past me; not an angry sound, but a keening despair. Her face is red, her tears fluent. She looks so sad. She has lost something. David Tudor keeps on playing.

So does the memory of that woman in my mind. I have come to realize what she thought she lost. She thought she had lost her Mozart, her Brahms. Only yesterday they had been streaming from the very air, and everyone was saying yes. But today, sitting with her friends and peers listening to the crazy-making deconstructionist bleeps and blops, she has to say no because she has lost the ability not to say it—much against her sense of decorum and fairness, I'm sure.

Thirty years later, I am still intrigued by the Stockhausen piece that so flipped the woman out, but when I think of her my heart is torn. Her holy place had been carved with graffiti. The devil had taken the virgin. Dissonance had won out over consonance, and her wails, sailing over it, are in my ears still.

ھ

In North Indian raga, there is a special concept for notes that don't belong in the scale. They are called the enemy of the raga. Dissonance is thereby partially defined as what does not belong. But enemy notes are often included in the composition on purpose because, as my teacher says, "When the king is powerful, enemies may exist without fear in the kingdom."

ھ

Relative to one another, dissonance is *ouch*, consonance is *ah*. The parlor-trick piece "Chopsticks" is begun on the piano with two fingers at once. The resulting two-note pair, F and

G, struck six times, is thought of as dissonant; the second pair, E and G, also played six times, as consonant. The ouches beget the ahs. In Baroque music, dissonance is carefully placed so that, as in "Chopsticks," it always gives way gracefully, smoothly, to consonance—something that we, as acculturated listeners, have come to expect within that style.

We think of Bach as being an essentially consonant music, but actually only about 75 percent of it is consonant. Close examination reveals a great range of dissonance hidden inside. If you play through a Bach piece omitting the consonance, the dissonance, exposed like bone, sounds like twentieth-century music—some unrelenting Shostakovitch, perhaps. Properly nested, dissonance complements consonance. But when the dissonance is exposed and unrelieved, the dichotomy is overthrown. The function of dissonance, like the function of noise in a big city, must then be reinterpreted. I live out in the country now, and it is quiet enough to hear the cows walking through the grass in my neighbor's pasture. But when I lived on Seventy-second and Broadway in New York, I loved the city. I loved hearing the utilitarian stream of sound I was part of, and wouldn't have traded that compression for any cow country.

The tunings of the metal bars of the gamelans of Bali are at best marginally consonant, and sometimes the overtones that mix with other pitches and overtones seem to border on chaos. Listening to this over a long period is brain-loosening in a special way. One day, you see the light of the island in a way you never saw before. "Oh," you say. On that same day your village gamelan sounds perfectly natural.

ح

For a lot of us, though, certain music just goes too far. There are those who insist, for instance, that heavy metal music is dangerously aggressive and painfully loud. Similar claims are made against rap and free jazz and atonal music. But the truth is that every aggressive music is assuaging someone's deepest fear. No matter the style, you can hear the terror of alienation. In much rock there is a heaviness so sucked and drawn that it must be shocked into light—plugged in and cranked up. What is heavy sinks to the bottom of the world, it is true, but the sound of metal shines. Weighted strings can shimmer like light from a singing sword. Underground, a diamond is still a diamond.

Music is the mirror of our deepest longing. When you hear violence in someone else's music, you are hearing that musician's best effort to work out the longing to belong, even if it may not be the effort you would exert, or any belonging you might identify with. Underneath the harshness is the struggle for wholeness.

How to imagine the diamond in the dark, the brilliance of Buddha nature inside a denigrated body? How to hear with compassionate ears when your ears are being bombarded?

If Music That Goes Too Far bothers you, first turn it down, put in earplugs, keep your distance, protect your body. Second, consider that although the musical language seems distorted and deformed past your limit of recognition, it is nevertheless a language formed and ordered by agreements among the players and the listeners. This is true for every kind of music, close to home or half a planet away.

Loud rock isn't the only music people find obnoxious. Much contemporary concert music uses its intellect as a weapon. Behind a glossy screen of elegant intellectual procedures, the composer's hatreds and love-hungers battle for their lives. It's half war, half dance. As a listener, you have to be patient with the war part and search for the longing in the dance. Give yourself a chance to understand that all music tries to be beautiful on some level, and tune in to that desire.

It is all too easy for our notions of consonance and beauty to fossilize and institutionalize into safe art: nonconfrontational symphonies and ballets where we can comfortably fall asleep. Sometimes it pays to listen to harshness. The absorption of musical dissonance teaches us to develop a compassionate response to the anger of rap and the drowning cries of overly mental composition. Beneath the fury a rapper says, "You can't live without me." Beneath the arrogance a headbound composer says, "This pressure in my brain can't be all there is—is anyone out there?" Each speaks powerfully of a loneliness that without the music would be even less bearable.

The hardest thing is to realize that the terrible darkness in music is your own darkness exposed. That doesn't mean I have to spend fourteen dollars to hear someone play out my darkness. But it is a kind of *playing* out, and the thing is the play, and the playing of music is not war, not quite. This perception may not fix much in this noisy world, but if terror music is stalking you, it may help you let it pass.

Healing Music

CALLING MUSIC "HEALING" doesn't mean it is. Often it wants to be, or means to be, but doesn't really know how to be. Soothing music is nice; gentle, spacey music is nice. Yet such music, and music that suggests journeys through the elements or through your psyche (however mapped), may or may not be healing. Only to the degree and in that quality that a musician is healing himself or herself through the music can a listener be healed through it. A fancy correspondence to the geomancy of Egyptian pyramids won't work, or to astrology, or to numerology. The Dorian mode won't heal you, nor will any other mode just because it is ancient or revered.

What does heal? Human resonance. Music isn't a pill. It is an exchange between souls. The Dorian mode is capable of carrying a musician's energy; so will any other. If I play for you and heal myself, you can be in that wholeness regardless of mode or musical scheme. Invoking the planets or the elements or the chakras cannot defer responsibility away from my human agency. The magician has to internalize the magic so that the magician *is* the magic, not simply the administrator of its form.

The way I see it, good music is healing by definition. What it means for music to be good is that it is whole, holy, holistic; good music is sane sound, sound sound. My problem with the term "healing music" is that by specially designating my music as "healing" I suggest that other music not so labeled is not especially healing. The characterization becomes clubby and prideful: my music has an inside track on what healing music *really* is. My advice: consider music to be healing by how it truly heals you, not by what bin it is in. Otherwise you might miss something that is genuinely healing for you just because it isn't in the healing bin.

What I consider to be healing music does not necessarily avoid dissonance; it may well be fueled by pain. But it is balanced by love. It may be blown by a crazy wind, but compassion is the rudder. It transforms slavery into shouting blues, oppression into the hard joy of free jazz. Healing music brings you in from the isolation of the wild to the companionship of the hearth, not through an idea, but through the sound of musicians who are themselves crossing over.

Poison Music

I AM IN THE FRENCH ALPS with two hundred Americans and Europeans at a summer Sufi camp across the gorge from Mont Blanc, well above Chamonix. It is 1971, a wonderful time of discovery for many of us. The explosive light of the 1960s has turned into the exuberance of devotion and spiritual practice, and in the air is a wave of new music. Many songs of praise are coming through, as well as new forms and techniques of music making.

One of our new ensemble practices is to sing the name *Allah* at top volume, letting our voices range freely over the tones of a chosen scale. A rendition might last for a full five minutes of interlocking breaths, during which we whirl like dervishes, or for a single exhilarating chord of harmonic roulette. Our skulls tone like bells. We become air that is itself alive and breathing. We call this a Free Allah.

On this day in late spring, thirty of us decide to take an alpine trek in the melting snows above the camp. We wear spiritual whites, colorful scarves, and mountain boots. Locked in step, we ascend shouting, "O! Life! O! Truth!" in Arabic. Our guide knows the way (he did this yesterday), and soon we are well above our tiny tents, chilled and steamy, dizzy and grounded, stoned by the sharp air and the towering, looming God-work inside of which we feel small and complete.

We come to a cirque, a giant bowl scooped out of the rock by an ancient glacier. The steep sides above us are thick with snow and ice. It is my idea to sing one breath of a Free Allah and listen for the echo. We all stand facing the opposite rim, agree on the seven tones of the scale, and let forth. "Allaaaaaaah!" The sound is orgasmic, but the echo is even better. Our chord comes back to us like the wake of a boat we have hurled across the glistening ocean of snow and stone. Many choirs ricochet from the granite galleries. We sing another chord and again the cirque sings. We think it is the craziest, juiciest human sound ever to resound from a mountain.

The echo gets better with practice. We even imagine we hear our vibrations coming back to us as a kind of human scream for God. Yes, there it is again. But wait! The scream is in French! One of the Europeans says, "Look over there—that line of dots. Mountain climbers."

Sure enough, not quite a mile away and halfway up the slope, perched on a steep moraine, are six black coals in the snow. We sing a Free Allah to them over the great spaces. This time the French in the echo is words, words we can understand. "Arrêtez!" they say. "Pour l'amour de Dieu! Arrêtez! Arrêtez!"

Our guide says, "Gee, maybe they're afraid of an avalanche," and suddenly we understand—such sounds can indeed loosen the snow and send it hurtling down. The climbers are yelling at us to stop our mountain music. They are begging for their lives. We watch for a little while, standing quietly with fingers pointing and eyes straining. Then, thoughtful and subdued, we turn back down the mountain.

No one can tell you what music is or is not. One man's meat is another man's poison, as the saying goes; what I know today is that one man's cosmic chord could be another man's white death.

Music does resist definition. It seems to want to be able to form itself according to where it goes and the work it does and the energies it conjoins. That's okay, we don't need a definition to be able to do something.

What I have learned, though, is that whatever music is, it is somehow round. Singer, listener, and song are arcs of the same circle whether you can see all of it or not.

Concert Music, Sky Music, Wedding Music

WHEN YOU LISTEN TO MUSIC, it goes where no one else goes but you. It reverberates in a chamber so secret that even you can't go there without giving yourself special permission. You keep forgetting the password, then remembering it. But once you are in that space, it is utterly yours, more protected from other people than the central cells of your brain.

And yet . . . you go to a concert where three hundred souls are listening to a Beethoven string quartet. No one moves. Millions of people have sat in millions of rooms listening with exquisite concentration to this same old piece. Are we all hearing, in our immaculate privacy, the same music? Do we all fiercely own the same experience? Are we one or many?

Then we walk out of the concert hall and say stupid things: the cellist looks like a vampire; the Largo was too slow; it was thrilling. Yet the souls of strangers touched, and something joined that we can't say, at least not to strangers. At least not face to face.

❧

On the Fourth of July we go en masse to fireworks displays. Like music, fireworks are ephemeral constructions that hang in the sky and heighten our senses. They reflect the same designs we see when we have our orgasms or rub our eyelids: neurochemical discharges from the rods and cones of the retina. Our most intimate signals are turned inside out and spread among the heavens. Self as illuminated cosmos. The boundary between our interior and collective knowing is transcended in a series of ecstatic moments. We go *ooh* and *aah* again and again. Under the umbrella of a patriotic holiday it is OK to enjoy our secret hedonism—and with a bang-bang-bang, at that.

Music is more subtle. It also projects our interior selves outward into what is collectively heard, a sustained moment during which we are all located on both inner and outer coordinates, all together, as one organism. *Ooh,* very private. *Aah,* very public. *Ooh, aah, ooh, aah.*

જ

A wedding joins separate families into one family. Listening to music is like a wedding ceremony where everyone gets married to everyone else. Every member of the party has the same desire: to turn into the music, to live as the entwined vibrations coursing the space in this split second. When the ceremony is at its peak and the magic has broken loose, every beat in every bar says: this is who we *are*, this, this, *this* is who we are, on and on, in every stroke.

5

What a Composer Does

Composition as Self-Expression

M Y Sufi TEACHER (or *murshid*, a Persian word) died in 1971. Within a month people had begun reporting dreams and visions:

"I saw Murshid last night. He told me to tell everybody to watch their feet."

"He told me to brush my tongue."

I am not expecting or seeking such visitations when I pull up to a residential curb one October evening in 1973, twenty minutes late for a prayer meeting. I quickstep up the front walk and into a tiny entrance foyer full of shoes and umbrellas. Then I stand very still because I am caught in the web of a special sound.

Through the closed door to my left I hear my friends singing a devotional song. The music has two layers: one layer is an Islamic chant, the other is a contrapuntal complement I had written to it a year before. Recognizing my own contribution to this praising sound at a moment I am feeling guilty is a redemption. I relax, untie my laces nice and slow and place my shoes neatly at the end of a neat row of shoes. "How nice," I think to myself, "to arrive after a hard day's work and hear my friends singing my music."

The foyer is suddenly lit from the top by Murshid's image. He is slapping his knee like an old geezer who has just heard a good one. "He thinks it's *his*," he calls down, pointing a finger at my head. Blackout.

I am left alone in the little room, but something has changed. The music sounds different. It is washing me clean. All sense of ownership has boiled off from it. The voices raised in polyphony have become hollow, sonorous, anonymous, and eternal. When it is finished I enter the prayer room feeling invisible.

Craft

W HEN I SPEAK about what a composer does, I mean what
I do as a composer, of course, but also what I can infer
by observing other composers and studying their music.

There are as many ways to compose as there are composers. A mother calming her child with a pleasing new song is as
certainly a composer as was Gustav Mahler, who may have
used reams of paper and an entire orchestra to commensurate
effect. Polkas, rumbas, ragas, and rap are all composed to various degrees in their various ways. Groups of musicians, especially jazz and rock musicians, compose collectively and refine
their work through performance. The ceremonial music of the
Balinese gamelan seems to be composed by almost the entire
village—dozens or hundreds of players over many generations
have their say in shaping a given piece. The strange process of
a lone individual single-handedly composing and notating a
piece of music, thus freezing its form for others to reproduce
later, is an act of Western hubris that causes some folks from
other cultures to scratch their heads, shrug their shoulders,
and—well—grin. But in our culture, the write-it-down composer has been cast as a hero, often a tragic hero, misunderstood, disdained in his time, and poor as a church mouse. This
characterization is due largely to the commercial romanticism
of a century ago, yet the popular image of the unhealthy, cur-

mudgeonly, debt-ridden, garret-dwelling bachelor does persist. What a composer actually does in terms of craft seems to most people an especially inaccessible subject, an unattainable understanding. So we have projected onto the composer a quirky antisocial persona that ripens, like cheese, into lionization after he is dead. An author's craft is just as difficult to master, and just as specialized; but everyone in the world has a spoken language, so the craft of a truly fine author, though it develops just as rarely in the population as the craft of a truly fine composer, is not perceived as alien. What a composer does for a living is thought of as an exclusive, perhaps threatening, magic.

I can see why. What strange mind would think to organize the sounds of wind and water, birdsong and human cries, to collect and shape and systematically quantize them? Yet such a mind is not strange. Indeed, part of the wisdom lost to our civilization is that the systems involved in music making are not separate from ourselves—they are reflections of the way we are designed to hear. As a people, we don't know that. We think composition requires special capabilities and initiations. We think it is for a chosen few. It isn't. It is for all people who want to develop their sensitivity to sound. Just as an author's craft develops through sensitivity to language and meaning and a painter's through sensitivity to light and color and line, so, as one becomes more aware of mere sound, the secrets of musical composition open like petals. So first and foremost, a composer trains to listen.

But listening is not enough. What is heard has to be remembered. Training to remember well can be just as rigorous as training to listen well. If you want to compose, you need to hold pitches and rhythms internally—at first snatches of them and then streams and rivers of them. You need to be able to freeze notes and phrases, dangle and turn them in the inner ear, shrink and explode them, and permute what survives. Learning the special signs for music notation is useful, just as writing is useful to an author. But music and literature both can be produced without knowing how to write, or read for that matter. You can dictate books, you can record music, and you can have someone else transcribe it later. On his deathbed, blind Bach dictated counterpoint to his son-in-law. The extraordinary polyphonic musics of Africa and Indonesia developed without benefit of notation. The live wire of North Indian vocal music is whole orders of complexity beyond the possibilities of its notation.

At best, notation is just a reminder, a glyph for what has been internally experienced. You have to keep it at arm's length or it will be like an obtrusive secretary who keeps you from getting your work done. It can hold you an unwilling hostage. There is no sadness like the sadness in the eyes of a classically trained musician who cannot play a note unless it is first presented as a dot on a page on a music stand.

But properly used, music notation empowers the memory. Properly, you write with the hand (Latin, *manus*). Maneuvering it, you manage to command your manuscript to manifest (all the same root). I am old-fashioned in that I write all first drafts (and most seconds) by hand, music and words alike. If the flow of sounds and images has not passed through my handwriting, the writing is somehow not quite real. Paper manufacturers (*manus* again) refer to the texture of paper as its tooth: good paper has good tooth. The tooth is waiting and hungry; it bites off the idea as it comes out of the hand, and that's how you know it is safely out of you and onto the paper. Your musical ideas are like the bugs that parent birds gather for their young. The chicks tug at the bugs and swallow them whole; the parents are satisfied and fly off to make another round. So we fly the rounds when good paper eats our writing.

Some composers write quickly and easily into their computer software, and I say go for it. But I have begun to notice things in such music that make me uneasy: glibness and overwriting. As notes become ever cheaper, economy of means becomes inflation of means. Should the use of hand be mandatory? Truth to tell, I love to shove words around in a word processor. Once the core ideas and images are drawn from the psyche in longhand, they have become so much syntax to be polished and tuned, and they don't get riled at being turned into pixels, which suit them. But musical notes linger in the hand.

So you can learn to hear internally, and to remember what you hear, and reshape it, and extrude it into dots and wriggles outside your skull. You can also, by dancing and tapping and pounding on the world, learn all the rhythms that attract you. And you can learn, by studying old music, the history of your ear. And you can learn, by studying harmony, to combine tones and combinations of tones. And you can learn, by studying polyphony, to render clear and distinct the layers of sounds. By studying orchestration you can learn to get the instruments and the players of instruments to produce the sounds you hear. But most of all, you can learn, heart to heart and mouth to mouth, the actual sounds of the music you love, its dialects and coded inflections, its secret messages that never appear on any page, its hidden moves between the notes. You learn this by listening.

You can learn all this within a few years—five or ten, perhaps—and be able to produce the material from which pieces are made. But the making of a piece—a long, whole, satisfying piece of music—takes more than a few years' investment, more life. Sooner or later you ask yourself the crucial question, "What is this a piece of?"

What Is It a Piece Of?

A COMPOSER WRITES a piece of what? One might say it is a piece of cobbled material, a piece of pieces, like a quilt. Pattern, color, and shape have to be considered, compared, selected, and stitched together. In its title, Sonata for Oboe and Piano announces its primary selections. From all available forms, this one; from all available timbres, these. The composer has scanned the culture's material and snipped out specific patterned fragments to work with.

But "the composition" is also a piece of the composer's history. When I compose, my piece is part of a stream of musical thought that began when I was a boy and will go on until the last trumpet blows. I cut a length from this long string of ideas, a piece of work corresponding with a piece of my life. When I hear it later I am as likely to say, "That was the year Lucy was born," as, "That is a twelve-tone suite for saxophones." It is a piece of the action selected from a life of activity. Just as one human is a part of human history, and one culture part of the history of cultures, so a composer's piece, to think more broadly, can be seen as a precisely cut fragment of cultural history. It is easy to see Beethoven's *Eroica* Symphony or Elvis's "Blue Suede Shoes" in this light. One's own piece can be seen likewise.

For a longer view, include prehistory. In their book on

microbial evolution, *Microcosmos,* Lynn Margulis and Dorion Sagan regard organic memory—"life's recall and activation of the past in the present"—as a basic condition of life. We are our own biological record. Most of the atoms that are in your body now weren't there ten years ago; they are transients who will give way to more transients. What remains is the pattern of stuff, which remembers itself. The stuff comes and goes. The pattern is tenacious over eons. You can escape the past no more easily than you can—ultimately—escape the present.

I live on the human frontier, a few miles from the Pacific Ocean in northern California. The Modoc and Pomo tribes lived in this area for thousands of years; it was disturbed by European explorers only a few hundred years ago. In London or Bombay or Cairo, you can put down your foot anywhere and be reasonably certain that underneath it are human remains, and beneath them, more human remains. My land lies ten miles north of the most northern known Modoc settlement and ten miles south of the southernmost Pomo camp. There are places on my six acres that may never have known the touch of human feet. This gives me a feeling of open-endedness, of being on the cutting edge. And my music feels most usually that way to me: I can write anything, unfettered and unbound. We are American pioneers, still squinting into the western wildness. But we have an unexplained longing, like astronauts whose radio contact with their disappearing planet is taking longer and growing weaker.

In India are masses of people with the eternal sadness of serfs, nothing like the restless anger of our freedoms. So bound are they to the past that new structures look ancient the day they are built. Lichens are integral to the design. Shapes are rounded and worn, colors are muted. Only the sacred colors are bright. Indian music seems to grow right out of the earth, and be whole with it. Ragas go back for millennia, reminding us in their endurance of the chain of microbial evolution unbroken from ancient sea to modern brain. The people of India might be rooted to the ground, but they are realized in their rootedness. A raga is a piece of extremely long history. Out in Sebastopol, I twist in my private paroxysm of past-shedding. Gypsies long for what they don't have: home. Hence the poignant longing in the New Age movement, a high-altitude grasping for what must be down there on the ground, or in the past, or in tribal life, or in cellular symbiosis, or in—God save our language—*networking*.

So our music is striving for independence and symbiosis at the same time. This is the aesthetic climate in which American composers specifically, and the composers of modern countries generally, write their "pieces." They didn't worry about such things in Bali fifty years ago. Pieces simply arose. But once you have modern*ism*, the dichotomy between past and present arises as a troublesome conundrum, an obstacle course. Nowadays the young Balinese musicians who are shaping the new gamelan pieces are listening to Michael Jackson and the sound tracks of television sitcom reruns and trying to figure out where they belong.

ℰ

Some words, like *cleave*, also mean their opposites. *Piece* can mean not only to carve out but also to stitch together: all of a piece, uniform, homogeneous, stable, and whole. In music, we say, "It's a piece," when we mean, "It's complete." The wholeness of a good piece of music resonates with the search for wholeness in our lives. And we do search, not just as individuals, but as groups, societies, and—with apparently increasing awareness—as a species. This book rests in your hand. There is something in my mind that wants itself in yours, and something in yours that wants itself in mine. Your eyes keep moving over the words, a million words from a million minds seeking one another. We collectively seek what is common, the ground where we all stand, and a common arch over our mutual understanding.

What if our collective mind just as earnestly sought communality with *all* of life, not just human life? Further, what if that collective life sought communality with all of being, transcending the duality between "life" and "being"? Such is the case, I think. A good piece of music functions as a micro-universe that we can see all of at one time, hear all of in one sitting. A good piece is a resonating chamber for our seeking of wholeness; its wholeness reassures us that we are not deluding ourselves in the search.

Nothing as elegantly balanced as the Mozart Clarinet Concerto, for instance, could be part of a universe that is not of a piece. As I listen, I can relax into the darkness as well as into the light. I won't be swallowed up; I won't die. I can cry if I want to, and laugh at the same time.

So a composer tries to compose a piece of the greater communion, a piece of the unity, a piece of one-ness.

When you try your own hand at this, your sensitivity is heightened and tested at every turn. You learn new responses to the old ways and means, to your own stream of musical consciousness and to your tradition and history. Your music matures as you become sensitive to what is whole-making in human experience. You learn, finally, that devotion to and absorption in all being is not separate from the act of composition.

☙

I have been viewing the composer in the more or less traditional light of one who decides what others play and how they play it. Deconstruction, in the ideas and music of John Cage and Cecil Taylor, for example, has long been afoot in the land to melt down and recast working assumptions, but seems ultimately to have the effect of retooling and remodeling rather than razing and bulldozing. Composed music as an agent for feeling whole constantly needs new definitions and new material to work with. The more adaptable and spry and exchangeable is the stuff of the body, the more the spirit inside has a fighting chance to live.

Discovery, Prophecy

MUCH COMPOSITION TAKES PLACE in the semidarkness, in a perplexing weave of light and shadow, certainty and doubt. You mustn't get stuck there. You must keep slogging because in this game the slogging actually generates the shining, as if you were pedaling a treadmill that generates light. The time will come when your composition feels totally right, free of struggle, as if the whoosh of waters had been waiting only for your signal. On those days your piece clicks on like the lights of a city. In the blaze of certainty, everything goes right.

The flow of these rare moments is not inward to self-congratulation, but outward to the thrill of discovery. You become convinced that, far from having invented your piece, you have discovered it alive and breathing beneath the overburden, a buried truth about us all, not so much a composition as an achievement in anthropology. This is the same truth I sense when I listen to Bach and hear—really hear—not only all the notes, but the whole scheme at once. Like a diamond brooch, this stuff has been both mined and cut. Who knows how it came to be underground or how long it was hidden there; Bach found it and shaped it.

When these fleeting moments occur in the composition process, the sense of self expands into the sense of Self. The identification that begins with "Who am I?" soars into "Here I am!" The piece writes itself within a sheath of light; indeed, the world lives itself. Your will and the will of the universe are the same. Everything seems effortless, if only for a few bars.

Beethoven's music has been described as proceeding "inevitably." The Fifth Symphony, for instance, seems like it was presented on stone tablets. Part of this quality may be an implication of musical composition itself. Musical terms and processes go beyond the dualism of language and reason into a realm where the verities of distance and time are played with like doll's furniture. We are rendered a vibration so fundamental that even with our speck of a brain we can snatch a piece of the wholeness, glimpse the one-ness of being and nonbeing. In the sense that prophecy is cosmic awareness as revealed through human agency, great music can be prophecy.

I know that I am not Bach. I also know that each of us can learn to mine and shape arduously his own work. When we do, glinting pebbles keep sprouting up mysteriously through the bedrock, or rolling in on the surf, turning up, randomly it seems, between our toes.

Writing It

W HEN YOU ARE WRITING a book, in that first trimester,
when the meaning and shape are still hovering spirits,
every word you read from every source seems pertinent. Reci-
pes, advertisements, critical articles, cartoons, everything is
fodder. Lines get underlined, pages dog-eared, clipped, and
filed; the files bulge. So it can be when your piece of music is
first forming. All sound—and the silence inside the sound—
streams in to nourish hungry ears. But you are also cut off,
isolated and aloof, a genius in the attic, a fool on the hill. You
sit alone in the dark hearing the muses sing only to you. You
hear everything, yet you are locked up inside your skull. You
become a sound nerd, possessed by nonthought, taken by a
world of notes and harmonies, obsessed with combinations
and sequences, with textures that recede as you reach for
them.

It's so easy to get lost in it—to leave your laundry lying
about and lose your watch and forget to wash and be drawn
up dangerously close to the sun. Perched on the fence between
inner and outer worlds you direct the traffic into and out of
your piece. This goes on even when, especially when, you are
not actually writing down notes. You are using what you hear
continuously, whether you are thinking about it or not. Everything sounds, especially your feelings. Your anxieties and exal-

tations are presented not as pitches and themes but as textures and timbres; states of feeling produce states of sound. From dark and gold patches of the psyche are extruded the rhythms and pitch combinations you will later smash and reassemble.

This might be called inspiration, I guess, but inspiration doesn't actually occur when it seems to be occurring—it has been incubating for a month of Sundays before you've got even a sign. Music might seem to come like a bolt from the blue, but the blue isn't just a nowhere, it's the very sky you've been walking under. What comes out of the blue has already been remembered and forgotten many times. It's just that it's now being remembered in some spiffy new form. But try as you might you can't turn these bolts on by your thought waves or by your wanting.

When you are composing a piece, you are living between the manifest and the nonmanifest worlds. Not quite all of you is in either: if you get lost in the blue your piece will starve. If you feed on too many ideas too soon your piece will take the form of an obese and stubborn child. To the question, "What do you do for inspiration?" I say I live in a good climate and get enough sleep.

∾

As your new composition gels, you learn to hear it variously. You hear it subjectively, from the inside, and identify passionately with its feeling and its meaning—there is never enough reveling in its heart as your heart and its mind as your mind. But you also learn to listen objectively, from a cool distance, as if you were everyone else listening to the newcomer's music. So one set of ears listens as you earnestly conduct the orchestra, exhorting it to produce the sound of your soul, while another set of ears is perched in the last row of the balcony listening with detachment.

Of all the lessons to learn, this is the most difficult because both the conductor onstage and the listener in the balcony must believe in the truth of what the orchestra is playing. It doesn't matter whether this is your first composition or your five hundredth; as the piece takes shape, at some level you become absorbed in the drama between what is personal and what is universal. Though you may have developed a thousand formulas and strategies, you never learn this lesson well enough, because the boundary between yourself and the collective self is evanescent and fitful. What is the difference between a personal confession and cultural catharsis? Between private pleasure and universal joy? Between coded metaphor, meaningless to anyone except you and your friends, and a crucial message everyone needs to hear? Each note and phrase must satisfy both sets of ears. Doubt creeps in. How, after all, could you be conscious from both perspectives at once?

We have models to help us—Mozart, the village *griot*, early Miles. But the models will take us only up to the doorsill. We have to breathe ourselves out into our own world. I guess this is ultimately why composers compose: to apprentice the position of midwife between self and all.

e•

The fight for objectivity begins with a stopwatch. A painter knows the size of her canvas before she begins to paint. Likewise, a composer knows how long the piece will be, or at least makes a clear guess. So composers struggle to learn how long ten seconds actually lasts, and thirty seconds, and a minute, and five minutes. A three-minute piece is different from a four-minute-and-fifteen-second piece. A twenty-minute piece has its character, just like an eleven-by-fourteen-inch photo enlargement. A forty-five-second piece is a postage stamp, a two-hour piece a thirty-foot fresco. Everything in between has its temporal identity, and you learn how to separate this from your body and from your feelings. A fifteen-second passage of music takes fifteen seconds to listen to, regardless of how much time and passion you've put into it.

Once I was at a symphony rehearsal with a composer friend whose piece was being performed that evening. At one point during the run-through, my friend became agitated; his eyes popped and he rose in his seat. Then he sat back, relaxed, fanning himself. He saw me looking quizzically at him. "It took me two weeks to write that bar," he explained. The joke isn't that he agonized over one bar for two weeks—that is expected. It's that he couldn't separate the fragmentation of his composing process from the real-time continuity of listening.

Each new piece you write is an opportunity to know time, your medium, fully awake and cooly detached. Eventually, by knowing time, you learn to suspend it and to zoom it and, if all goes well, to leave it behind.

Some unsolicited advice to the composer-in-doubt: choose a piece of someone else's music that seems quite perfect to you. Then pretend you wrote it. Identify with the composer so completely that you can hear every bar as though you yourself had composed it. Just pretend. You'll probably find yourself nitpicking the great infallible master. Try Mozart, then late Beethoven—a string quartet—then Bartók. Just try it. Then try asking yourself at every turn, "Is anybody going to actually get this? Is it coming across?" Across indeed. When Bird first learned to play like Bird, in Kansas City in the late thirties, the singer he was backing up turned around and said, "How can you be playing that *shit* when I'm trying to sing?"

But it is dangerous to try to hear your own music as others might hear it. The uneasy feeling will steal over you that you are playing to the balcony, and those ears can take over. The music will become too easy, maybe cheap. A struggle breaks out. The conductor says, "Listen to me! It's *my* soul!" Ostentatiously, then, the listener in the balcony yawns. And so the balancing trick goes on. It is written into the act.

The most helpful thing is to be able to hear your music live, in actual performance. The fantasy then becomes true— what was a private tussle is now a public event: the performers are playing your piece and you are listening in the balcony. You can never fully understand the balancing act until this day is lived through, the more times the better with as many pieces as possible. This is the way your music learns to become both subject and object, as it must, completely, in order to be useful and survive.

ନ

So your precious composition teaches you, finally, about the unity of opposites. You learn to be hollow, and yet to be filled with Siren song, following it where it draws you. You learn the reciprocity between trust and discernment. You learn how to be in the crowd and how to take a bow. You learn that to be common is to be chosen. You learn how what is most deeply your own belongs to everyone.

Pleasure in the Long Cycle

THERE IS A FINE SERIES of drawings and poems from ancient China called *Ten Bulls*. The drawings, each within a
circle, are titled:

1. The Search for the Bull
2. Discovering the Footprints
3. Perceiving the Bull
4. Catching the Bull
5. Taming the Bull
6. Riding the Bull Home
7. The Bull Transcended
8. Both Bull and Self Transcended
9. Reaching the Source
10. In the World

The first six drawings depict a calm little man absorbed
in various attitudes toward the bull. In Number 7 the man is
sitting outside his house, but the bull has disappeared. Number 8 is completely empty. Number 9 shows a river and flowers
but no little man. In Number 10 the man has returned with a
paunch, and his possessions are slung over his shoulder on a
stick. He carries a jug and looks like a Buddha. "Everyone I
look upon becomes enlightened," reads the commentary.

When I was twenty-six years old, newly serious as a composer and casting about for compositions, I lit on the idea of an instrumental setting of *Ten Bulls*. I chose about a dozen instruments for my small orchestra, wrote "Ten Bulls" on the cover of my sketchbook, and set to it. Number 1, "Searching for the Bull," was easy: Galumph galumph. Sniff sniff. Stop and squint, dart forward, then off to the side, stop and look around. Number 2 was also easy: *Aha*, a something—is it the bull? No? Yes?

Number 3 was a bit more challenging. What is *actually* meant by the bull? Yes, I knew it is your own self, your ego, of course, but however would one set that to music? I finished composing it even though it seemed a little confused. Number 4 was more perplexing. What's it like to catch yourself? Long passages were written and x-ed out. I wrote a few bars, left some pages blank, wrote some more. Well, when you're stuck, go on to the next problem.

Number 5 also was tricky. Best to leave it and go on. Number 6 seemed easier because, you know, there was a flute in it: the little man was sitting on the back of the bull, peacefully riding it home while playing the flute. No problem. I wrote that. Though when I read back what I had written it didn't seem real calm. Why didn't the picture and the music match?

Number 7 should be simple: religious music. So I started out with some Gregorian chant–sounding ideas. But by that time the hollowness of it all could not be denied. I asked myself, "What about Number 8—a silent movement?" How stupid. Maybe this wasn't such a great idea. I put the piece on the shelf and started another, for a similar orchestra plus a soprano, called *Songs of Celebration* (1966), which got itself completed.

In the early 1970s I found the Ten Bulls piece and read it

again. By this time I was a Sufi initiate and thought, "Hot dog! I can finish this piece now, I'm a Sufi." So I started to fill in the blanks of Number 4. And I started again on Number 5 and I trashed the old Number 6 since it was obviously immature. Then I laughed a lot because I saw how the Ten Bulls are a metaphor for inner realization and how could you compose it if you didn't have it? So I put the piece back on the shelf, deciding I could forget about that one.

Twenty years of North Indian raga singing later, I've looked at the piece again, and once more have got interested in working on it. But this time is a little different. I don't want to finish it. I want to be finishing it. It's a lifelong piece, added to as I am added to. Now, instead of a chore, the piece is full of humor for me, like the original drawings. Lifelong amusement.

Erased Music

I

After a life of looking, a proper pencil
appears, WOODBINE by EMPIRE No. 2.

Sharpen twenty at a time by hand
on a crank sharpener that says CHICAGO.
Line them up with the loose graphite wiped
and blown from the points. Keep the erasers
out of the sun, and don't press down too hard.

If the point breaks once too often,
murder that one, enjoy the crack,
hurl the parts across the room
where they can lay till cleaning day.

For a wrong note or errant dot
the eraser of an Empire will suffice.
Sometimes whole bars have to go,
entire passages. For these
get a one-inch Magic Rub.

I will sometimes erase a full page
as a moral act, my right forearm

in wide sweeps of rectitude.
I know it's good for me
but I hate these blunders.
"You are a perfect human," Devi calls
from the couch where she's reading
while the other end of an Empire
mops up the hollows and grottos
where Magic Rub could not go.

The two ends of a pencil are Shakti and Shiva.
Writing and rubbing out, we want
balanced lives. Show me the nub of a pencil
with an eraser still fresh
and I'll show you mindless charm.
But the unused length of a pencil
with an eraser worn to the rim
is some critical soul still waiting
for perfect inspiration. Both ends
must diminish in harmony and die
like lovers with the same breath.

II

Through curtains of quiet air
luminescent notes are wriggling up
into your throat: lantern fish
and now some deep-sea squid.

Down the arm to the fingers bits of glyphs,
the *punctum* burrowing through the lines
scratching quick slants and spirals
out from a black spring. The heads fixed
with stems get quick with beams,

proud with flags, calm with ties,
glossy with slurs. "Rub it out,"
yelled my fourth-grade teacher
every day in the same rage: "Rub it out!"

Under a ten-power lens, the passage revised,
revised again is a city ruined and opened out
by wars that no one now comprehends.
Rubble and sticks every which way
houses and churches you can see down into.
I love the look of smudged pulp
and torn fiber. I ask my student
to run a finger over the roughest place:
"See how my piece is coming along?"

Fighting the Dead

I HAVE NEVER FELT so *understood* by anyone as I have by Mozart. He anticipates my needs. I need to breathe; he knows when. My mind needs time to rest; he knows how long. He gives me assurance that it is spring, even on April days when I am lying in green grass. In the big universe, faith flickers, dimming and shining by turns. In the little universe of Mozart's music faith is constant. No *Is the ship sinking?* No *Am I burning away?* Only *This sound is true.*

My experience of Mozart's music is part of my everyday present, my aliveness. It prompts my love and goads my work. More than once I have come to a crisis of self-knowledge needing a real answer to a real question. That is when I listen to Mozart and have a good cry. Then I know who I am and what to do.

Mozart is at once my ideal of perfection, my inner voice, and the ancestor who nurtures me. But he is also my rival. What jealousy Salieri was supposed to have had I also have had, and have. It is a station of the cross, an albatross, and I wrestle with it. Probably many composers do, the ambitious parts of them, anyway.

From the gallery of great composers, Mozart, Bach, and Beethoven especially are the ones to beat, and they will beat you every time. Even though the issue is fruitless and constrictive, one still is haunted and tormented by the unimaginable excellence of these musical minds. Why write second-rate music? Why add to the bins of lesser works? There are obvious answers—your culture needs you; you are not competing with the dead; you are working out your own salvation, etc.—that assuage reason. But your vulnerable part curls up and whimpers. Surely most composers outgrow these pains, but they are part of the learning game. At some point we want to kill Mozart.

The point is, of course, to transcend the sense of rivalry. I tried two ways. The first was to make Mozart into my actual historical father—I feel I've *lived* him physically as my father—so that I could oedipally and compassionately dispatch him. For decades I've been preoccupied with the historical details of Mozart's death scene, which was, in fact, sufficiently grisly and common for me to accept that he was a mortal like me and that he did die. Same with Bach dying and Beethoven dying.

The second way is to hear him. Nobody could profoundly hear Mozart and remain jealous of him. That amounts to being jealous of yourself. When you go past the pilgrimage, the seeker becomes the sought. Really experiencing the music wipes clean the rivalry, just like real devotion washes away duality.

Bach Dying

Sitting up in bed, benign, blind,
an old organ chorale running through his brain
he is dictating revision to his son-in-law.
Lord, When We Are in Direst Need
has yielded to *Before Thy Throne I Offer This.*
"G natural in the tenor, now the soprano D,
dotted, and in the alto . . .
That's enough. Come back tomorrow.
Same time." He leans back and dismisses
with a wave his seeing eyes, his writing hand.

He is alone for now, and let's just say this:
Gabriel has not arrived. God is a day's journey.
Sebastian is about to have another little stroke—
only a moment of clear hearing left.
At the foot of his bed an old serf
dressed for the fields is revealed holding a flute
and searching Bach's face for a sign.
Bach can suddenly see the man's eyes!
He loosens, strangely content, very tired.
"Play some simple music," he says but then
there's a hazy whoosh: finally, too much
blood in Bach's brain.

Or this (no one knows anything anyway):
Bach wakes up and sees a very young man,
limbs heaved into the bedside chair, composing
a love ballad. His passion makes a puppet
of him and his flung hand barely strokes
a string on the lute in his lap.
It is that same G of the tenor, an offhand
twang that rides out the window
and up into white glare.

The day I read that when Bach died
he had eleven shirts at the laundry
was the day I began to hear him
enough to learn him. Jesus breathed
and sweated. Bach got his shirts dirty.
It wasn't the Passion of St. Matthew
or some hymn lifted through the diapason
that he went out on, but the chance note
of the young lover he had been, a G,
midrange, that I could learn to sing.

So That's What We Do

MARILYN HAS STUDIED with me for five years and she wants to take a break. She is a psychotherapist who works with dreams and music and is one deep cookie. This is her last lesson "for a while," she says, all teary-eyed. We hug. I hear my next student turning into the driveway. Marilyn turns to go, then turns back, "By the way, Allaudin, I heard your music on the radio."

"Oh?" People report this from time to time.

"It was on 'Morning Edition,' during the Gulf War, a year and a half ago. I was lying in bed. Ordinarily I know enough not to listen to the news either in bed or in the morning, but these were extraordinary times. I heard of bombs and death—just stupefying cruelty. Then your music came on, for only twenty seconds, but it was enough. I lay back and sank into it. It cleansed me and took me completely away, and when I got up I realized I didn't have to be in denial about the news." She turns to go again, turns back once more and says, with a laugh, "I just had to tell you that."

As she walks down the path greeting the next student I think to myself, "Oh. So that's what we do."

☙

In 1989 Devi and I go to Thailand as tourists, staying with a family in Chiang Mai as part of an exchange program. The husband, Boonlert, teaches agrarian resources at the national university. He and his students travel to remote villages and show the farmers how to increase their yields and be competitive in the world market. Would we like to come on his next round? Yes, yes.

The following day we drive fifty kilometers into the countryside, an Asian bounty of forests and fields spread out like green emulsion between sky and rock. The village chief greets us and shows us into his house. He is young (forty-five) and compact like an ultralight plane. He chain-smokes unfiltered cigarettes, as do many of the other men. We sit on the floor around a huge open tablecloth, eating sticky white rice and spicy water buffalo meat cooked with medicinal-tasting vegetables. Everyone is spacious and gentle and generous, nodding seriously. They are incredibly present. The men talk farming.

ↄ

In 1974 I had been introduced by a friend to the music of the Shona people, an indigenous population of what was then colonial Southern Rhodesia, struggling to become the independent nation of Zimbabwe. The friend, Paul Berliner, has lived with the Shona, studied and recorded their music, and written a treasure book about them. Shona music makes use of layered cross-rhythms. Not only are the layers going at different speeds, but they converse in such a manner that the ups of one are the downs of the other. This music is to rhythm what Bach is to counterpoint, namely, the apotheosis. The Shona play it on what we call "thumb pianos"—elaborate constructions of metal prongs housed within large hand-held gourds and played with the index fingers and thumbs of both hands. The instruments, held sacred, are called mbiras (em-*bee*-raz). The Shona sing to their ancestors and gods accompanied by an mbira ensemble. The music drove me wild and energized my work. I learned to adapt it to the piano in my own way (I call it mbiano music). Evidence of it and homage to it is woven into all the music I have produced since.

In 1987, when I was recording the album *Available Light* for Windham Hill, I was also working on a forty-eight-note mbira pattern, attempting to play what at first seemed an impossible combination of rhythms. Will Ackerman, my producer, heard me practicing it. "What's that?" he asked. I told him. "Record it," he said. I did, five full minutes of it, unadorned—one hypnotic pattern over and over meant to accompany some singing. He loved it and kept coming back to it. "Let's put it on the record." "OK." But I was uneasy. "It needs something. Singing, but not me." "Who? Name the person." "Well . . ." I was too shy to say who I wanted, but I did anyway: "Bobby McFerrin." Will called him. We sent him a tape. Bobby listened and agreed to try to sing a melody to my mbira pattern. One afternoon in a San Francisco recording studio, he did so. It made us all cry, every last listener. We put it on the album and released it with many thanks to him, and my friend Paul, and the Shona people and their ancestors and their gods. Bobby, incidentally, at that time had never heard of mbira music, or the Shona people. He just sang.

❧

Now our Thai village lunch is over and we are about to go out into the fields. I want to thank the chief so I pull a copy of *Available Light* from my pack and present it to him: "My music from the USA." Boonlert translates. Without a word, the chief and his men troop out to the village pickup truck, whose dashboard houses the village cassette player. They light up after-lunch cigarettes. The doors of the truck are flung open; men lean and slouch and narrow their eyes. The chief sits in the driver's seat and pops the tape into the slot. This is a factory-new tape; the mbiano music with Bobby on it should be buried halfway into the B side. Miraculously, though, that's the piece that is cued up: we hear a few piano notes, then the ageless lift in Bobby's voice. It floats up through the cigarette smoke and over the green foliage. The men look at each other, then down, listening. There are nods, a few words. Intense listening. I can feel the spirit of the music curling up out of Shona village life, up through my friend Paul's teaching and my long hours at the keyboard, up through Will's quixotic attraction and Bobby's transcendent singing. And I get the strange sense that the Thai men are hearing all that too. A singing thread is being stitched around the world.

Now the piece is finished. Very serious nods, simple words. One by one the men find my eyes and give a sign—a thumb up, a little smile. No Western smiles here, no exclamations or compliments, just confirmation: *What we just heard is true for us.* The chief neatly pockets the tape and walks away.

"Oh," I think to myself, "so that's what we do."

6

Sound Is the Teacher

A FEELING

FOR

NUMBER

Abundance

I AM LYING AWAKE with my eyes open. In the near dark are familiar shadows: the folds of curtains, the forms of furniture. I am a peace-loving man in his own bed, but when I close my eyes I am ranging an unfamiliar, lighted vastness, plumes of star stuff and radiant molecules. I am an X-ray a billion light years long, phosphorescence under the surface of the sea, a boy in a movie cartoon, a window in a cathedral. *How could I be here in all of this?* Out in the kitchen a floorboard creaks—*my* kitchen. How could I ever *not* be here? It makes no difference where I travel or where I stand, I cannot imagine my own life or death.

Tonight I have become uneasy, roaming inside the powers of ten, lost in the boundless abundance. How could there be so many replicated layers of being? The generosity of the host is an embarrassment. I am a musician and there is no music in the infinite. Infinite *potential*, yes, but nothing you can hum. No lullaby. Before I can fall asleep I will need a fix on my position, a glyph I can decipher, a formal garden to tour, a strap to hang on, a map I can read. Please tell me where I am before I swoon altogether. Inhaling gingerly, I gather myself in from the flung worlds. Exhaling, I sing a low baritone note, scarcely louder than my breath, but sustained and steady; as it tails off I can hear my heartbeat in it. This tone has tamed infinity. It has organized my energy, centered my mind, dressed my desire in a dimension I can recognize. It is a house I can safely enter. Now I can fall asleep, and I do.

The next morning, with the sun on my tablecloth, I think back to the night before and wonder what all the fuss was about. Now I am surrounded by objects that are hard, colorful, and useful. *How could I be here in all of this?* is replaced by *What's for breakfast?* Last night, music was a blurred face through the window of an express. This morning it hums through my head, homey as a pot holder.

Most folks think music is spiritual and etheric, and it is, but it is also palpable and concrete. It bridges the infinite and the finite, the subtle and the coarse. Sometimes when you come home from a day in the trenches you need the subtlety of music; it releases you from the denseness of the earth. But after lying awake at night in the ocean of being, music becomes something you can touch, a mooring, welcome ground. A sung tone, like a thrown rope, can rescue you from the universe.

Long Tones

Nature is restless. It loves change. Long unwavering tones are hard to come by in the wild. Sometimes the wind's whistle might find a certain note it was searching for or a coyote's howl rise to a plateau before it inevitably falls. Though there are other exceptions—ringing in the ears being the most pernicious—the tones of nature generally teeter and totter planlessly as a tightrope walker's balance pole.

Nature avoids straight lines, also. If you were a wild hare who escapes predators by zigzagging, would you trust the rails that slice the prairie? Straight could mean dead. If you were cumulus, wouldn't jet trails give you the creeps? An unwavering line or tone must be shaped by a discriminating mind, and seems to be the intentional mark of human beings. A straight road through a forest is all business.

We ring bells in order to broadcast a human message. If you have ever been alone in the country and heard a church bell from a distance you know the glow that comes with the sound of your own kind. The complex harmonies remind us that we can refine metal and cast it in geometric shapes and release that purity as vibrating air over miles of buildings and trees. The sound hangs in the atmosphere, metal suspended in air: human magic.

Early on, as a twelve-year-old trumpet player, the practice

of "long tones" was a despised constraint. I resented those breaths of rigid pitch-making and the weekly homilies of my trumpet teacher: "You'll *never* get *any*where if you *don't* practice *long* tones." When I tried, my lips would tire and my mind would wander. By the third note I would already be miles off in the woods or down the hall.

At first it does not seem natural to play an unwavering tone on a blown or bowed instrument, or to sing one. To fight entropy, you must engage your mind and your will moment by moment, be critical and aware and centered on the inner world of sound. If you are a violinist, unwavering means steady bow pressure and a relaxed arm stroke. If you are a flutist it means breath control and the perfect placement of your breath stream. Your whole body is involved in a balance of tension and relaxation, and your ear is making a continuous comparison to a standard of nonfluctuating pitch projected in your mind. A long tone is not a single boring event, but a stream of perfect moments. You must be determined to straighten nature, and nature will test you without remorse: "Why not run zigzag like the hare? Save yourself!"

Now, after forty years of learning to sing long tones, singing them defines my life. They tell me I have a brain that works, ears that hear my voice, and—somewhere—an ideal of perfection. Now I am addicted to this habit of singing a breath's worth of a deep note. I sing "Baum" or "Om" in private, rounding the corner between the hallway and the kitchen, or softly at the grocery checkout line. I sing a slow, low "Baah" or "Chaow" to remember that I am myself, and more than myself. I love the way I can monitor the line between wild and human. Maybe I need this practice to prevent my psychological annihilation, to keep my person from flying apart and disappearing entirely.

To discover this sound mirror for yourself, you can first

try humming or singing a long tone that *isn't* unwavering, that falls with gravity. Then you can make the tone rise and fall like the wind on Halloween. Then finally you can venture a tone that holds steady against nature. The fluctuations of a pitch are as easy to recognize as the wiggles of a line. When you do hear yourself singing in an unwavering pitch you can hear your own intention reflected in it.

It is comfortable to begin with a hummed *nnnn* and then open to *aaahh*. The more open the vowel, the more strength and concentration it takes to straighten the wiggles. Notice how the intimate *nnnn*, which resonates mostly in the head, opens into the exposed *aaahh*, which resonates in the chest. You can keep the closed sound a secret, sitting calmly at a committee meeting while others about you are losing their minds. With *aaahh*, however, you are an extravert, exposing your flank, opening the tube of your body to the surrounding air and the world beyond it. There is a time for *nnnn* and a time for *aaahh*. However you sing them, long tones are seeds sown in the space you move through. The musical life germinates from spaces like these and grows leafy.

Firefly Constellations

IN THE THAI DUSK, fireflies are twinkling in the bushes and trees of the riverbank. As the darkness thickens, the firefly flashes appear more intense. The timing of the messages at first seems random, but not for long—in the tree directly in front of us a pattern emerges. Neighbors coordinate signals. A small covey on a lower branch becomes synchronous, then a large group above flashes in opposition. A baffling electric intelligence fills the eye. Within a half hour the branches are black against the night and the entire population of male fireflies has found its collective pulse, about one per second. In silent, bright unison, the tree is lit with communal intention.

The firefly phenomenon is a rarity in animal species, though not in cells. The pacemaker cells of the heart, for instance, agree on the heartbeat (Selah). By firing in synchronous arrays, the neurons in our brains enable us to feel and think. But collective rhythmic behavior in nonhumans is sufficiently unusual that when it does occur we are amazed and entertained. We marvel at the timed acrobatics of birds navigating the wind; we pay good money to see the leaping choreography of dolphins. I am not referring here to mere reaction, as when a herd of deer bounds away from a rifle shot. I'm talking about animal rhythms that make our human jaws drop and our eyes squint. Certain moths will mate only when their high-pitched tones match perfectly, like lovers in an opera. Animals are not supposed to steal human thunder. That is the stuff of animated cartoons—beavers playing drums with their tails, honeybees dancing the soft shoe—and we laugh because animals are doing our stuff, and we know they can't, not really.

Collective rhythmic behavior is so integral to our human routine that when we witness it, or participate in it in our own lives, we take it for granted. I want you not to take it for granted, at least for a few pages. I want you to feel rhythmic unisons and, eventually, pitch unisons, as the everyday miracles they are. I want walking in step together and choruses of "Happy Birthday" to be celebrations of how far we've come.

We are especially chary of mobs and gangs these days— they so stunningly act out our collective fear. But not to forget, in our caution, the immense aesthetic radiance of human unisons. On with the marching band, on with the square dance, the connectedness of symphony orchestras, the precise wildness of cheerleaders, the patriotism of national anthems, and every other expression of our collective good.

Human Unison

A N ICE AGE FANTASY: A woman and her three-year-old daughter are alone in a cave. The child, in a high fever, moans low in a drawn-out voice. She closes her eyes and discovers that whenever she fixes her sound in one place, like a goose flying straight rather than a looping swallow, she feels better. The mother is inhaling the girl's pain, trying to cleanse it. As the woman exhales, she meets the rhythm of her daughter's breath, and matches her daughter's voice in her own throat. She closes her eyes also, and the unison moan goes on. Two bodies are one body. When the mother opens her eyes again, the daughter is smiling.

Another prehistoric fantasy: On a windy plateau six men are waiting in ambush. Hidden behind small trees and tall brush, they are excited but quiet. They want to murder the five men who are far off downwind, moving toward them. It is bitter cold. To keep his mind from jumping out, one of the waiting men makes a shivery rumble in his throat, hardly audible beyond his own bones. Then all six men are making the same sound, gathering courage to avenge ancient wrongs. They are singing a war song.

True story: In 1944, during the dark days of World War II, my second-grade tap class learned a unison routine for the popular hit song, "When the Lights Go On Again (All over

146

the World)." We all had flashlights with different-colored gels over them. During the performance for the PTA—which meant our mothers—there occurred one of those moments that stay vivid for the life of the brain. At the apogee of the dance the house lights went down, the flashlights went on, and there we were, a class of dancing, singing, multicolored beacons of hope. I was borne along by the single stage-body of swinging arms and black patent-leathered tapping feet. I became the human body, fighting for and against itself, the body of the war, of the winning of the war, the body of Good. We had worked hard for this synchronicity, and now, in front of all the mothers in the world, I found my collective, light-desiring self.

Also I remember counting to one hundred in unison with the entire second-grade class. We built up toward each nine-ended number a fine tension, which we released energetically into a zero-ended number: twenty-six, twenty-*seven*, twenty-EIGHT, twenty *N-I-I-I-N-E, THIR*ty, thirty-one, . . . We rode those nines like incoming waves, surfing them sensually, beyond any number learning.

℮

Too much togetherness can be threatening. Though we learn by mimicry, we abhor mockery. *Make Sally stop making fun of me!* Even worse than mockery is the specter of an uncontrollable, dark-sided other, a doppelgänger. Imagine: some stranger appears and mirrors your actions and speaks in unison with you; a mirror you can't shake off. Yikes!

Just because behavior is collective doesn't mean it's good. Rude forms of synchronous action are easy to find. As long as folks identify through attack and defense, marching armies will heighten that identity. When the army belongs to the other guy we can smell the fear, and the wrong.

Walking in step is not for armies alone. Some of my finest times in life are walking the country hills and flats with Devi, swinging our limbs together, clapping in unison a forty-eight-beat wedding dance rhythm Hamza El Din taught us. Nevertheless, the beneficence that arises from the sustained rhythms of dance and song develops slowly and fitfully (like most things), as human spirit evolves and as the need arises.

Not until I paid attention to what goes on in an orchestra was I struck by the evolutionary nature of human unisons. When I was in college I heard the Chicago Symphony perform Beethoven's Fifth, which all the players knew by heart. About a minute into the first movement there is an especially intense, jazzy violin unison which, in that performance, was a true unison of sound and spirit. The violinists—about thirty of them—leaned into the stream of notes athletically as oarsmen. The fingers on thirty left hands were pressed onto fingerboards in precise agreement measured to the millimeter and timed to the millisecond; the bowing of thirty right arms, connected by the composer's music, made visible the unseen. I was exalted by what Beethoven had received, by the tremulous leaps, by the spirit that drove his life and his culture, internalized by these violinists a century and a half later and now given out as a shout of triumph. I saw how humans have learned to share energy in intricate and immaculate ways.

എ

The truest human-to-human unison is in singing. When two people sing the same note, their vocal cords walk in step. But instead of legs moving back to front a couple of times a second, the vocal cords move back and forth a few *hundred* times a second, escalating the sensuality from earth to floating, aural space. Two pairs of ears can tune two voices together so fine that the two people can seem to disappear into one another.

I say "seem to." No one can control his voice completely. No sung tone is utterly unchanging in pitch, volume, and timbre. A singer can never quite throw down the tightrope walker's balancing pole. He is pursuing a center of tonal gravity that is itself alive and moving.

But when a functional unison—close enough for human binding—does occur, there is a lift inside it, a bonus for oneness, the added dimension of resonance. Resonance is not a metaphor for a good world—it *is* a good world where energy appears like a messenger telling us that we are among friends, not separate, and not nuts.

ℰ

When I go to Pandit Pran Nath's house for a singing lesson, his soft "good morning" is followed by a wordless nod toward the tamboura leaning up against a corner of the room—his signal to tune the instrument and begin the lesson without further speech or delay. In this he appears not like an aloof teacher but like an intent lover who cannot bear the small talk before the embrace. I take off my shoes, sit opposite him, cross-legged, on the floor. Even before I am finished tuning, he has sung the first phrase, which I then repeat.

This routine—he sings, I respond—is reiterated many times. Each time, after the first few seconds of my response, Guru-ji joins me in the final notes, not so much to correct me or shore up my memory as to blend our voices in true unison.

Usually, the unison is not quite true. But if I'm having a good day, and understand the raga a little bit, my voice will become gentle and silky like his. In the shifting colors of the

melodic line I cannot find my voice or his. We are both cam-
ouflaged; it is a disappearing act, a reprieve from my striving
student self: guru grace. The acoustic boosting that happens
when waves entrain creates a resonance more subtle than
sound. During these lessons the plain living room is imbued
with a floating, unattached light. Riding on sound like this I
am certain that my teacher knows my heart, has known it all
along, and has given me exactly what I need this very morning—the right notes with the right qualities and intensities—
to further my unfolding. Love is thus refined.

ॐ

The rich resonances of human unisons are available to everyone, yet only the tiniest fraction of our lives is spent actually
experiencing them. Unless you are a monk who chants in a
monastery, or a professional chorister, or a symphony string
player, the bonding of unisons is easy to lose and forget. Perhaps we are still wolves and whales, prowling for mates, howl-
ing for territory, wary of invaders, protecting our wavelength
and resisting the true unison. Much as I love loving my
teacher, I too am wary, fearful of mirrors. It's hard enough to
be myself, much less melt into anyone else. We want independence and we want union; we are caught between solo and
unison like a feather in the grass, quivering for whichever
we're not.

Yet a few breaths of unison with a friend can be green
islands in your day that are so quiet you can hear all the way
across the ocean. You can ask a friend to sing a long, even
tone, which you then match—a full breath's worth. This is
perhaps easier with a same-gender friend, but if you can han-
dle the octave difference between men's and women's voices,
gender won't matter. If your friend is more secure about

matching a pitch than you are, you sing first and have your friend match you.

You can do this a second time, each with a hand on the other's shoulder. Then on the next turn, if you both feel like it, looking into each other's eyes. And on the next, touching foreheads, being one bone.

Composite Sound

E XCEPTING LOVE, nothing is simple. Nature contains no such thing as an undecorated chain of waves, no single layer of sound. Sounds that seem pure—an angelic voice, a thrush, a chime—are actually busy societies of interwoven vibrations. Even a pure sine wave electronically produced will not be heard as pure; once you hear it, it is part of the ear, and the ear adds its own complexity to the signal. This complexity is the nature of nature: waves make waves.

Any slice of creation will vibrate if you strike it, or bow it, or holler into it. The ensuing vibrations—even from an object that *seems* to be all of a piece, like a guitar string—are actually nested layers of ever faster (and ever smaller) vibrations. The reason there are so many levels of vibration is that matter naturally divides itself into segments, smaller and smaller connected fragments, in various configurations according to its form. Each separate division of the object produces its own chain of waves—the smaller the segment, the smaller (and faster) the vibration and the higher it sounds to us. Taken together, the sum of these sounds illuminates the object's inner structure, its hidden canyons, propensities, and singularities.

Next time you bang a pot lid while working in the kitchen, notice how the sound it makes is actually many separate layers of sound. There are, in fact, so many layers of sound in the lid that it seems *wherever* you place your concentration, high or low, you will find an independent bell-like tone there, as if each of the night stars were ringing. In order to scan the layers you need to be mentally active. This analytical wakefulness is what musicians spend their lives training and polishing. It is an intellectual act to notice that what seemed to be one thing is now many things; it whets the appetite for understanding the microstructure of the everyday, and gives you a fine buzz.

Scientific research is becoming increasingly sensitive nowadays to the mutuality of macro- and microworlds. Galaxies cannot be conceived without quarks. Astronomers and particle physicists are talking earnestly with cosmologists over lunch. Likewise, musicians are being led to new forms and new meanings by a rekindled interest in the micronature of sound. The pot lid can be on the cutting edge of your own (privately funded) research.

Every sound you hear is stacked vertically in layers and stretches forward all the way to inaudibility. When you listen for this depth and breadth you become all ears, but of course you can't hear it all. You can't taste it all either, or see it all. In the black spaces between the stars are the stars we cannot see.

Why organize a universe this way? Why did God invent matter that divides and divides again? And sound that makes our ears long for more sound? I've heard that God used to be all of a piece, an infinite colorless homogeneity. But the night grew so long and the music so boring that, as an alternative to lonesomeness and boredom, God made the various worlds. That's why now there is plenty of good company even in the wee hours, and tasty food, and something nice to dance to.

Octave Mystery

DURING MY fiRST YEAR of college, my roommate, Al, showed me how to produce overtones on his guitar: while plucking a string with one finger you lightly touch a special place on the same string with another finger. If this is rightly done the voices of angels ring out. When the touched point is exactly at the middle of the string, the overtone is one octave higher than the tone ordinarily produced by the string. Al pointed out that one-half the string length produces a tone of twice the frequency, an inverse proportion. Hence, what is called an "octave" above a tone is actually twice the frequency of that tone.

By this time, music had been my passion for a decade. I thought I knew a lot about it since I was, after all, a budding composer. At the moment of my belated octave discovery, I had two intense responses. The first was a flash of cranial fireworks fit for such an epiphany. The second, as the flare fell, was the feeling that I had been cheated. How could I have come this far as a musician without having *realized* such a fundamental musical truth? Why hadn't anyone told me?

The key is "realized." I'm sure I had stumbled somewhere across the fact that an octave equals double the frequency, or noticed how string players produce harmonics by touching their instruments. I was, in fact, a practicing trumpet player, hour after hour racing up and down the overtone series of my golden tube. Nevertheless, I had not internalized the significance of the octave as the herald of musical organization until my roomie off-handedly enlightened me.

I found out later I wasn't alone. When a child first learns music, she typically asks, "Why does low C sound the same as middle C except different?" Or, "Why does a scale start over again an octave higher?" These questions, usually shrugged aside with "That's just the way it is," should be taken seriously; such a moment is the teacher's opportunity to reconsider the question herself—to reenter the mystery of musical essence.

Let us, as adults, go over this again. When you sing a scale up through the seven named notes (A, B, C, D, E, F, G), the eighth note, named A again, sounds like the first A, except higher. The two sounds are the same and different. Same name, same "note" (whatever that is), but higher pitch. When a man sings nursery rhymes with a child, he is singing precisely the same song, but lower than the child. They are singing together, but they are singing apart.

There is something easy in the harmony of two tones an octave apart—played either separately or together—but an octave transcends *easy*. There is a way in which the tones are identical. How can this be? Exactly what *is* it that is the same?

There are two ways to answer the child's query. The mathematical-acoustic one—an octave is double the frequency—can be framed according to the student's intellectual capability. The psychoacoustic one is far more challenging: it is that we don't intellectually know, that it is a mystery at the heart of music. One could point out, however, that listening clearly to a simple octave may lead us right up close to some huge thing, and that if we are sufficiently attentive we just *might* catch a slippery mystery by the tail.

The Rope Trick

THE BEST SOUNDS for study are the sustained vibrations of long metal strings, because we can hear the tones and touch the strings. But there is a problem: the strings move faster than the eye can see. Wouldn't it be nice to have a string that vibrates slowly enough for us to see each individual oscillation and scrutinize the magic of its division?

Enter the jump rope. A ten-foot length of pliable rope, at least as thick or up to twice as thick as a clothesline, can help us relearn something we knew as playground children. Attach the rope to a hook or post shoulder-height from the floor; or ask a coconspirator to hold on to one end. Wrap the other end around your hand once or twice and stretch the rope taut. Now give it just a little slack, then snap it taut again.

See and feel the resulting vibration. Assuming a more or less constant post-snap tautness, the rope will vibrate fully back and forth (or up and down—same difference) about twice per second. As it gives up its secret, help it along a little by moving it back and forth *at its own* frequency. (Your friend has to hold steady.) Thanks to your resonant help, the vibration will be more pronounced; you can see it and feel it more strongly. It feels good.

This vibration is called the "fundamental frequency" of the rope. It is the slowest and most integral of the various motions it knows how to make. By integral I mean that *all* of the rope, the entire length of it, moves to the right (or up) and to the left (or down); it is all of a piece. Empathize with the rope as if it were confessing something. The feeling you are getting through your wrist is a translation into motion of the rope's properties—its dimensions, what it's made of, its plasticity.

Practice until you can reliably elicit the fundamental frequency from the rope and, by the slightest sympathetic vibration in your wrist, keep it going as long as you like. As you feed this small but specifically timed energy into the rope, you get the impression that you are getting back more than your are putting in. This is the whole-body feeling of being in tune, the danced version of a sung unison. It is this slow-motion version that turns outward the inner meaning of sound.

Question: Who is the active one, you or the rope?

Answer: The active molecular forces in the rope are manifest in its oscillating properties, so the rope is active. But you are putting energy into the rope, so both the rope and you are active, each aspects of the vibrational essence of the created world. That's what we used to know so clearly in the playground when we were kids jumping rope.

Duple Nature

A T THIS POINT the rope wants to tell you more, but it is shy and secretive. Some cajolery is needed. If you let the rope's middle sag more than halfway to the floor, then rapidly move your wrist in a circular motion as if you were writing circles on the wall in front of you or turning a small crank, and if you time it right, and adjust the slack right, the rope will form into a sideways S, like this:

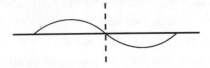

with a complementary peak and trough. Once you generate this spinning shape, snap the rope taut. Everything moves faster now, and the eye will blur these more rapid oscillations. For the few moments that the vibration continues on its own, two halves will seem to appear symmetrically at once. With some experimentation you can fatten and prolong the image. The whole thing will look something like this:

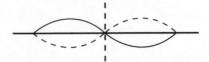

The vertical dotted line in each of the drawings cuts

through a point where the rope is relatively stationary. This point is called the *node*. It is the dividing point, the point of stasis relative to the rope's duple nature. A finger placed on that spot will not impede the vibration that is going on in each half of the rope. It is hypnotic to focus your eyes on the node while the rope is vibrating—it is the stillness in the middle of commotion that draws you in.

Each of the rope's two sections behaves like a half-size version of the entire rope. But the crucial difference is: each of the half-size ropes is vibrating faster—in fact, twice as fast—as the original, full-length rope.

You can know this three ways. First, it is logical, because it represents an inverse proportion, and inverse proportions are logical. Doesn't it make sense to reason that you can throw a rock *twice* as far if it is *half* as heavy? Or that each *half* of the rope will use up the energy of your wrist by vibrating *twice* as fast as the full length of the rope? Or that two times one-half equals one?

The second way is counting by eye. The fundamental frequency will vibrate about twice per second; in the duple division there will be about four vibrations per second. You can clock them, and compare.

The third way is by counting with your body. You are dancing with the rope. With your help it will get you jiggling twice for every once you used to jiggle. If you compare again the duple frequency to the fundamental frequency, you will feel baby steps to giant steps, two new ones to one old one.

Duple nature is no stranger to the body—your left and right sides tell you this. Walking shows our duple nature through time. Imagine walking. If every time you step on your left foot you say "Ho," then the relationship of the sum of your footfalls to your spoken words is two to one. Or, sitting down, count evenly, one, two, one, two. Tap your right hand on every "one" and "two," but tap your left hand only on each "one." Your right hand is tapping twice as fast as your left: two to one. Or, written as a mathematical ratio, 2:1. Back to the rope: when it divides into two parts, it vibrates twice as fast as it does when it vibrates all of a piece. It wants to show you the elegance of its duple nature.

Weeny Person

W HEN YOU LOOK at a movie or video in very slow motion you see a succession of still frames. Even at eight or ten frames per second you see a jerky series of stills. But at about twelve frames per second the eye's ability to discern discrete events begins to break down. At about eighteen frames per second the breakdown is complete, the jerkiness goes away, and the pictures blend into a movie.

The value of the rope trick is that it slows vibration enough for us to see the individual oscillations. We can even hear them individually, as a succession of soft whooshes. If the rope could go fast enough, at about twenty-four oscillations, or cycles, per second, the ear's ability to distinguish individual whooshes would break down and another perception would take over—the perception of pitch. But if we pulled a jump rope taut enough for that to happen, it would break. Enter the musical string.

The full length of the A string of a guitar vibrates at 110 cycles per second, which is a comfortable note in a man's low singing range. That plucked string is a blur to look at, but the sound of the tone is a clear, dark straight line in your ear. The same string in its duple motion sounds an A one octave higher, at double the frequency, or 220 cycles per second, a comfortable low note in a woman's singing range. When a man and a woman sing those two tones (or any two tones an octave apart) simultaneously, the vocal cords of the woman are oscillating twice, for every single oscillation of the man's. If you could *see* the two sets of cords it would be like your two hands tapping 2:1. What you *hear* is an octave. We sing octaves quite naturally, without thinking or knowing anything about it. How do we do this? Is it a trick?

It is a trick.

We have the rope trick built into us. Our ability to sing in octaves effortlessly—around campfires, in prayer meetings, with the radio—without being cognitively aware of the octave's duple nature shows the innateness of our harmonic ability. Music is the name we use for the outward unfolding of this nature. We do harmony because we are harmony.

When two listening people sing in octaves, the 2:1 ratio can become quite precise. It is like walking with someone while holding hands. If you walk in unison (this is the simplest case) your steps match, and you feel the synchrony of physically swinging together. If the other person takes nineteen steps for every twenty of yours, you spend most of your time out of phase, and the unison is out of tune.

Now what if the other person jogs two little steps for every one of your walking steps? He is jogging an "octave" faster than you are walking, and the synchrony can be clearly felt. But if the other person slows a bit, taking nineteen steps to every ten of yours, the "octave" goes out of tune.

The ear is fast and smart. Even when the vibrations are going one hundred (or one thousand) times faster than walking, the ear knows what is synchronous and what is not. Octaves are in tune when they are exactly 2:1, and human ears seek the purity of that resonance with the same hunger they seek the purity of a unison. They know this purity like the mother and her baby know the rhythm of their rocking. You have to make this conceptual leap: the baby in the ear is rocking *very fast*. This is the clue to understanding the psychological pleasure of musical harmony.

To the ear, the rocking does not seem fast. Ear time is as fast as fruit fly time. A fruit fly lives its adult life in one day. In ear time, 250 cycles per second (middle C on the piano) is a leisurely stroll down a lane lined with elms. A thousand cycles per second (a soprano's high C) is the gentle waving of a Chinese fan on a summer afternoon.

I think there is a tiny man in my ear, a proper cleric sitting at a proper desk with a proper notebook and an abacus. As the sound waves of, for instance, two people singing in octaves come before his desk, he counts them on his abacus. To his weeny self, only a few microns high, these waves are huge and slow, and quite comfortably countable. He says, "Oh, yes, very good. Do continue." When the soprano goes sharp, the little man says, "Too fast there, slow down." When the tenor goes flat, he says, "You, lad, speed up—*move* it. There! That's better now: two of hers to one of yours; very good, proceed." He can count two for one just as naturally as a glass rests on a table.

The swing of walking and the beauty of the musical octave are connected through the coolness of the numbers 2:1— the numbers form an arc between feeling body, hearing ear, and thinking mind. As we study more musical relationships, the numbers become more complex but the principle remains the same: we feel the numbers, and the numbers feel good.

Two Was Good

L ET'S RETURN AGAIN to the child's question: "Why does the scale seem to start over when it reaches an octave?" This is one of the finest questions no one can answer. Such questions have spawned a promising new field, psychoacoustics, which asks how we experience what we hear.

A word about the word *octave*, which means eight, as in *octopus, octagon,* and *October* (which was originally the eighth month). A musical scale can be seen as a ladder; in our culture there are seven distinct rungs in that ladder—seven scale tones—before the eighth tone of "starting over again" occurs. Culturally, we prefer these seven-rung ladders. But other cultures prefer five rungs in their ladders, so in those cultures, the scale "starts over" on the sixth note; an "octave" would be the sixth note, or a "sixth." One kind of music divides the musical ladder into twelve equally spaced rungs; in that twelve-tone system, the scale "starts over" on the thirteenth note—an "octave" would be a "thirteenth."

Regardless of how many rungs are positioned on their musical ladders, all human ears recognize the doubled frequency as the place for starting over. We simply do not know why everyone has the same subjective response to this objective stimulus. If enough people want to know, we will probably find out. In any case, our word *octave* is culture-bound, appropriate to the music we Westerners are most familiar with. "Twice-as-fast" or "2:1" is the proportionate—or harmonic—name for the "starting over" effect, which is common to all people.

So the power of the number two, at least for us humans, seems to be toying with the principle of *sui generis*, that which generates itself, not unlike life. When I lie awake and wonder about this, the wonder fills my house. It's as if God, before Creation, had the *idea* of multiplicity and made a go of it. But in that first created moment, God became suddenly conservative and said, "Let two be different from one, but not so *very* different—I don't want any trouble when I try to find my One Self in my Two Selfness." So God made two, and experienced it, and saw that it was good, that is, not too far out. God was content and felt at least the possibility of *considering* three, which we also will, presently.

I think if the octave question makes you sufficiently crazy, sufficiently frustrated in not being able to plumb it more deeply or embrace it more fully, if it exhausts your brain enough to lead you once more to the bare act of listening, then you *have* it: you are experiencing the underlying principle of musical harmony.

7

Sound Is the Teacher

MUSIC
APPEARS

Triple Nature

WE AND THE ROPE know how to get a lot trickier. If you let the rope's middle sag just halfway to the floor and again you make circular motions with your wrist, but this time somewhat smaller and quicker motions, and if you time these circles just right and adjust the slack right, you will produce a threefold division in the rope, with two nodes:

These vibrations—proportionally faster than the vibrations of the duple division—may be too rapid to count easily. The rope now behaves like three ropes, each vibrating at three times the fundamental frequency. You can compare threeness to oneness by going back to the original rope trick and experiencing again the frequency of the entire length.

Before considering what sound would be made by this thrice-as-fast frequency (if it were fast enough to be audible), let's spend a moment in the slowed-down, arm-and-leg world of sensible pulses and examine the response of our large, slow bodies to thrice-as-fast.

Count "One, two, three, One, two, three, One, two,

three, One, two, three." For every *one,* tap a finger of your left hand:

Say: *One two three One two three One two three*
Tap: *One   One   One*

Make sure your spoken numbers are evenly spaced (not One, two, three, *pause . . .*)

Now add to this by tapping a finger of your right hand as you speak each number. Finally, stop speaking and just tap:

Right finger: Tap tap tap Tap tap tap Tap tap tap
Left finger: Tap   Tap   Tap

You are making triple time, a waltz, which is as different from duple time as a triangle is different from a line. This threefold symmetry has puzzled and absorbed the bicameral mind ever since it realized that baby makes three.

It didn't always realize this. I love my dog, a golden retriever of modest intelligence. By running experiments on him I have ascertained that he can count to two. For instance, he can relate an event immediately to another event: a finger snap to the left, then a finger snap to the right. But, regardless of how I frame the problem of three, he loses count and has to start all over again. I try clearly intoning *He Ha Ho,* or conducting for him, impeccably, a simple Strauss waltz. I encourage him to pay attention and he tries hard, but he just can't get all the way through to three without losing his concentration.

I am not sure we are so very advanced from canine perception. I cannot sufficiently detach my body from its twofold symmetry to waltz without feeling one of the beats as extra. I do remember learning to waltz as a young child and having trouble toughing it out all the way to the third beat. I failed many times before succeeding, so as a tapping adult I don't take the apparent simplicity of a three-to-one for granted. The complexity that occurs after duality is not obvious.

In the enormous, creative leap from duple nature to triple nature, God abandons caution once and for all. In a duple universe, unity is safely tethered—one foot is planted on the sill while the other, all curiosity, pokes outside the door. In a triple universe there is no holding on, no turning back. The cat definitely manifests out of the bag.

From the number three come powerful metaphors for our inner life of thought and spirit. Lao-tzu, around 600 BCE, wrote, "One has produced Two, Two has produced Three." A commentator explains, "These words mean that One has been divided into Yin, the female principle, and Yang, the male principle. These two have joined, and out of their junction has come a third, Harmony. The spirit of Harmony, as it condenses, produces all beings." In music, the difference between a self-generating duple world and an other-generating triple world is both audible and illuminating, as we shall see.

This mind stuff becomes real through body experience. Let the feeling of the waltz guide you. When you are sure of your three-to-one tapping ability, you can use different parts of yourself to both give and receive the stimuli. Pat your left cheek three times as you tap your right foot once. Another way: while using your right index finger to draw the three sides of an equilateral triangle on an imaginary blackboard, tap your left foot once. Or actually waltz!

What would happen if you tried to express the three rhythm with down and up motions only? Then clearly there would be two downs and one up or, more typically, one down and two ups. This action gives a feeling of something extra. Which is the extra beat? If nothing is extra, then are the second and third beats equal, or is one of them naturally stronger? Try tapping One, two, (rest), One, two, (rest). Compare that with One, (rest), three, One, (rest), three. What *is* the hierarchy here? What does your body say?

If you try to get rid of the extra beat by going *Down,* up, down, *Up,* down, up, using up six beats to complete the cycle, you've invented an even greater and more fascinating complexity, but six is not fair game yet.

Now, if you go back to simple finger tapping and experience the pure thrice-as-fast with no ideation or truth searching, you will know, when you come back, what other dwellers in this realm have known. And you will be just as tongue-tied as anyone who has ever tried to describe it.

You can never learn this world too well, nor will you ever be bored by it. I don't fault my dog for not being able to count to three. It took me a whole life, including a million bars of waltz time, not to get lost.

A House for Sound

L ET'S GO PAST the tapping and past the rope into audible sound. The sound of three-to-one (3:1) can be closely approximated on the piano. If we choose the C below middle C as the fundamental tone, the tripling of that tone will come out to be the twelfth white note above it, called a twelfth: in this case, G above middle C.

Although any in-tune piano will give a good idea of the quality of the relationship of the fundamental to its tripling, it would be better to have a guitarist produce the higher tone as an overtone of the fundamental, or do it yourself if you know how. You could use the open D string, tuned down to C (for compatibility with this essay). The ideal way, however, is to sing the pitches with a friend, the higher voice a twelfth above the lower voice.

When you listen to the harmony of the two tones combined, you hear that, unlike the fundamental and its doubling, the fundamental and its tripling are essentially different from one another—at least more different than the same. This perception is worldwide: cultures that name scale tones assign identical or similar names to octaves (tenor C and alto C) but different names to twelfths (tenor C and alto G). The two tones C and G clearly belong together: they are placidly, eternally, and utterly consonant. But they are different specifically in that we do not perceive the musical scale as beginning again at the twelfth tone. We are instead in a different place, not born again but grown past our birth into a new creature. As we shall see, this newness grows new newness, and eventually a structure is built, a structure of tones—a house for sound called music.

I know writers cross a line when they ask readers to move away from the comfort of the reading position, away from the insulated zone of page-eye-mind, the precious unruffledness enclosing the lighted course of thought. I've tried to be a good boy so far, but now I'm crossing the line. Do duples! Do triples! Beat them with your limbs. Sing them with your voice. Internalize their qualities and compare them. Place the geometry of the soul into your physical body. Identify with their pure harmonies. Equate what they are with your response to them. *Be* with them. They are what you are, body and number both.

Gentle listener, don't be alarmed. Would I ask you to abandon your safe harbor precisely *now?* We have enough cruel writing as it is. But soon. Soon enough. Afterward, you can return to these pages about duple and triple nature and say how you did that part already.

The Powers That Be

THE QUICKER THE WRIST, the more the divisions of the rope. It will divide into four parts (with three nodes):

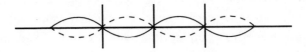

It will divide into five parts (with four nodes):

It will divide into six parts, seven parts, and so on, limited only by the length and constitution of the vibrating object (rope) and the nature of the excitation (wrist). Dr. Overtone's personal best, with a sixteen-foot rope, is a modest seven. An acoustic bass string excited by a bow well coated with resin can produce audible overtones corresponding to twenty or more divisions.

Although four is a fine number, it is not a prime number and so will give us no new magic. A fourfold division of the rope is, of course, a twofold division of a twofold division. The *left-right* of a march is still a march when you count *left-and-right-and*. Once again using the C below middle C as our fun-

damental, the fourfold division of that string produces a quad-
rupled frequency (4:1) two octaves above the fundamental, the
comfortable C of a soprano's midrange. An eightfold division
of this string (eight times the fundamental frequency, or 8:1)
produces, predictably, a note the next octave higher: the soprano's high C. A sixteenfold division (16:1) will produce the
flute's highest C. A thirty-two-fold division (32:1) produces the
highest C on the piccolo (and piano). So we see the powers of
two result in a series of octaves.

A piece of music starting on C and containing only doublings (or halvings) would have only Cs in it. You can find
every C on a piano and play octave music, like a kid who has
just discovered that there are eight Cs on a piano *and here they
all are*. It's an eerie piece. The stack of octaves sounds like the
shell for something, an outline with nothing filled in, the
floors and ceilings of an empty building. That is why the duple
world is considered harmonically sterile. It replicates itself
only; it does not know how to make a new realm.

The powers of three are different. Try using the *lowest* C
on the piano as the generating tone (calling it "one"). If you
count up twelve white keys, you beget the new note: G, the
tripling of the generating tone (3:1). Now starting with that G,
count up twelve more white keys, and you come to . . . Aha!
. . . D—*another* new note. This D is a tripling of the tripling
(9:1). Now starting with that D, count up twelve white keys to
find yet another new note, A, which is another tripling (27:1).

An infinite number of new notes is thus generated by the
powers of three—as many as we can use. The number three
can thus be thought of as fertile and creative; entire music
systems come from the tripling principle.

☙

Once you leave the safe, undifferentiated world of the unison, the powers that be are innately specialized. The powers of two open the space for music, but provide no music. The powers of three present us with vibratory states that reveal a creative nature; these we externalize in the form of musical tones exactly tuned. The sounds of these harmonies mesmerize us; we want to live inside them, move about within them hopping like toads, or gliding like raptors. We want to sing melodies that we make from them, and we do, because we are starved to know who we are, which is what the sound of music tells us.

Pentamerous Nature

FIVE IS THE NEXT prime number after three. Just as three is an entire world more than two, five opens a new, "prime" realm of experience that can't be defined by anything previous. I love the word *pentamerous* because it sounds like love (though it actually has an origin different from that of *amorous*). A few pages ago I was condescending toward my dog, who loses count after two. Well, guess where most humans lose count—right about here, between four and five. Quick, which has more syllables, *rehabilitate* or *similarly*? A *ménage à trois* is not difficult to imagine, but *ménage à cinq*?

Almost none of the world's music is in true five meter. Most of what's called five is not a true five, but an alternation between the lower primes, three and two. A true five is a pentacle, a pentagon, a five-pointed star. There is a whole phylum of truly five-natured beasts, called echinoderms, those of the spiny skin: sea stars, sea urchins, sea cucumbers. Cut an apple or a quince through its equator—you can fall right into the fivefold symmetry of the seed cavity. Let your eye be drawn all the way into the heart of a five-petaled wildflower. In pentamerous nature, the stability and purity of triple nature has been filled in and swarmed over by an exotic fullness we can feel.

Johannes Kepler said that you can account for the nature of fruit blossoms not only by contemplation of their beauty but also by contemplation of the number five, which characterizes the soul of these plants. "The fruit from a pentamerous blossom becomes fleshy, as in apples and pears, or pulpy, as in roses and cucumbers, the seed concealed inside the flesh or pulp." He emphasizes the especially fecund quality of five by noting that from a hexamerous (six-sided) blossom "nothing is born except a seed in a dry cavity." So it's fleshy fruit versus dried cavity, is it?

Human thought is permeated with the five mystery. There are five elements—earth, air, fire, water, and the fifth, quintessence, the spirit of all the others. There are five directions—north, south, east, west, and center.

One way of invoking pentangularity is to try to draw a pentagon with equal sides and angles, or trace one in the air. It is revealingly difficult:

Dr. Overtone tries to draw a pentagon freehand.

Nothing will ground you in pentamerous nature so much as beating, or trying to beat, a true quintuple meter. Complementing our duple symmetry, we have five-fingered hands and five-toed feet. Try tapping on a table top, one finger after the other, calling your thumb One, and the succeeding fingers Two, Three, Four, Five, counting smoothly and evenly. This is neither easy nor obvious, but if you stay with it you can feel your pentamerous self. (Be sure not to emphasize the three— One-two-*three*-four-five—or the four—One-two-three-*four*-five). As with every other musical element, the five-fold division of time appears out of vapor as a sudden presence.

More accessible, more accurate (but slightly diluted) is the practice of walking and using your fingers to number your steps one through five. As you get into the feeling of your walk, five nature will take over. I say "slightly diluted" because this is really ten nature. Every other *one* will be on an alternate foot, and ten steps are needed for the five-times-two cycle to come around. All in all, though, this is the best way to feel convincingly pentamerous. A refinement: slightly flex each finger in turn as you step, without even thinking number names.

The ancient cross-rhythm between two (legs) and five (fingers), still common in India and the Middle East, is less obvious in cultures dependent on wheels (not legs) and calculators (not fingers). This cross-rhythm is hypnotic and elevating; it keeps you spinning but grounds you before you spin away. It brings good fortune and beneficence, like our optimistic five-pointed stars. By walking in five you can bring back a lost time.

In the realm of musical harmony, pentamerous nature is the very face of beauty. If we choose as a fundamental tone the C two octaves below middle C on the piano, then five times that frequency is the E just above middle C (or the seventeenth white note, counting the fundamental as One). Play the two tones softly. Then play only that low, low C (the fundamental) and sing the E (in falsetto if you have a low voice), quietly mixing your note with the bass: pentamerous harmony. This tone is known in music as the third tone of a major scale, the "major third," the *mi* of *do re mi*. To associate it with the quintupling of something—its harmonic essence— seems numerically confusing even to trained musicians, since this crucial subject of harmonic proportion has so completely fallen away from our musical training. (This is discussed in more detail in the next chapter, "Naming the Tones.") But as with duple and triple harmony, quintuple harmony is made real by understanding the rope, by slow-motion experience (walking), by internalizing the vibrational experience (listen-

ing and singing) and by the little darting leaps we make between these different ways of knowing.

Monkey wrench: Our culture has gradually and conditionally traded the beauty of pentamerous harmony for another beauty, perhaps commensurate, perhaps not: the pleasure of being able to travel through many keys—of having
many different tonal "starting places"—within a single piece
of music. In our system, called "twelve-tone equal tempera-
ment," quintuple harmony is audibly compromised. To make
the system work, all of the major thirds on a piano are tuned
a tad sharp, not enough to drive you crazy, but just enough to
make you want to keep moving. So our music keeps moving.
One might call it restless; one *might* call it rest-challenged. I
say "conditionally" traded because when the music *does* calm
down and stay close to its starting key, sensitive singers and
players of variable-pitch instruments (like violins, not pianos)
adjust their quintuple harmonies to agree with their innate
pentamerous nature, and thus our ancient, patient ears are
recompensed.

The best way to experience pentamerous harmony, which
is, as we now see, a semi-endangered species, is to produce the
appropriate overtone from a low string and let that guide your
singing. Ask a musician who knows how, or read "Three Ways
to Produce Overtones" (two chapters hence).

I cannot really tell you how the beauty of an apple blossom and the spinning symmetry of quintuple walking and the
gorgeous harmony of "major thirds" are all allied, or explain
their qualities, or claim that they improve posture or cure sci-
atica. I can tell you only that this is the harmony that has
opened my heart, has been a house of beauty for one who
loves to live in beauty. Pentamerous harmony and the other
harmonies that stream from it have humanized the study of
music and given me to understand that music and my re-

sponse to music—what spins and my spinning in it—are the same.

Two opens the door.
Three opens the mind.
Five opens the soul.

Naming the Tones

Y ou catch a bird by putting salt on its tail. Names are salt. It is time to sprinkle names on these tone birds we have been chasing.

Consider the many terms of endearment we use for those we love: the honeys and sweeties and dears and darlings and pals and buddies and friends and flames and helpmates and soulmates and lovers we have in our lives. The musical tones we love have many names also.

Some names refer to the harmonic nature of tones, others to their melodic nature. *Harmony* means the relatedness of things through proportion and feeling. In harmonic space, musical tones relate through doubling or tripling or quintupling, or combinations of those, as in multiplication by small whole numbers. Such tones live together in resonant chords.

Melody, strictly speaking, is about linear distance, the way things are placed along a line, or in a row, like steps in stairs, which we count one by one. Tones are melodically related by scale steps.

If you made a piece using only Cs and Gs, the harmony would be fine but the melody would be poor—"ungrateful to the voice," a singer would say, because the voice proceeds most gracefully stepwise. Conversely, a mosquito's whining song forms a fine melody that has no harmony—at least not for us.

Say you have a loving grandmother who lives in another city. Now imagine that you are shaking hands with a stranger to whom you have just been introduced. At the moment of the handshake, who is closer to you, your grandmother or the stranger? Trick question, because there are different ways of being "close." You are made from the same genetic material as your grandmother, and you have familial love for her, but the stranger is close enough to touch you. Harmony is your grandmother in another city. Melody is strangers touching. Music is defined by the interweaving of these two kinds of closeness. The following diagrams try to separate them out, then weave them back together.

HARMONIC NAMES

Common Usage

The lowest and slowest vibration of a string is associated with wholeness or oneness, also with the earth. Its common name is "the fundamental" or "the fundamental frequency"; it is also called "the generating tone." The words *overtone* and *harmonic,* identical in meaning, are descriptive of the higher frequencies, but alas, both terms are cumbersome if used for *specific* identification. This is because the *first* overtone (or harmonic) above the generating tone is *twice* the frequency of the generating tone, the *second* overtone is *thrice* the frequency, and so on. So the proper number name of the overtone will always be one digit too small. We have the same problem when naming the years in the twentieth century, which are all numbered in the 1900s. Scientific language has

	The Whole Rope	Duple Nature	Triple Nature	Quadruple Nature (Duple again)	Pentamerous Nature	Hexamerous Nature (Duple and Triple)
GENERAL USAGE	Generating tone or fundamental	First overtone or first harmonic	Second overtone or second harmonic	Third overtone or third harmonic	Fourth overtone or fourth harmonic	Fifth overtone or fifth harmonic
SCIENTIFIC NAME	First partial	Second partial	Third partial	Fourth partial	Fifth partial	Sixth partial
RATIO WITH C	1:1	2:1	3:1	4:1	5:1	6:1
CYCLES PER SECOND	128	256	384	512	640	768
THE ROPE						

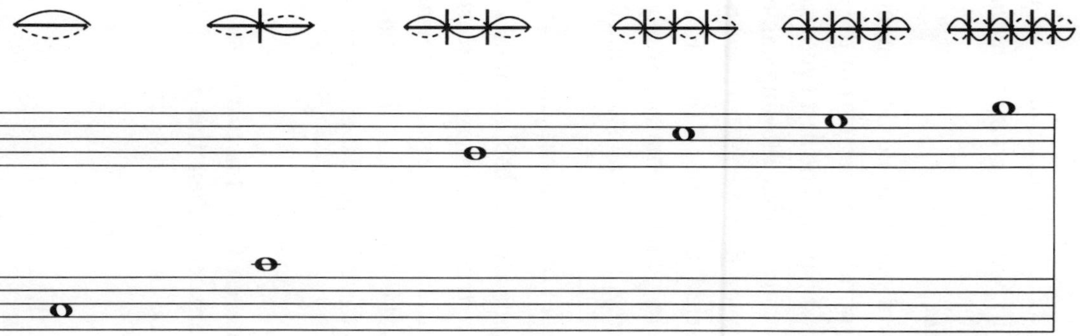

Figure 1. *Harmonic names of the overtones of C.*

solved the problem, however, by using the ratiocinized term *partial* in place of *overtone* or *harmonic*.

Acoustics

The word *partial* could be thought of as "part of the totality" of the sound. The first *part* of the sound, the generating tone, is the first partial. The first overtone, or the *doubled* frequency, is the *second* partial, allowing name and number to agree. This is the favored nomenclature, even though we cling to "overtone series" as opposed to "partial series," which sounds incomplete, perhaps tentative. Surely the name Dr. Overtone has a fine ring. Dr. Partial is unthinkable.

Ratio with the Fundamental

The ratios are the absolute names for harmonic relationships. They are true for humans the world over—we know this simply by listening to the music they make. Notice that the named note is the first term in the ratio, not the second. So, for instance, the third partial is shown as 3:1 (not 1:3).

Cycles per Second

If the lowest C on the piano were 128 cycles per second (it is, approximately) then the actual frequencies generated by it would be as shown in figure 1.

MELODIC NAMES

Letters

The alphabet letters reflect our culture's proclivity for scale ladders with seven rungs. An ascending scale starting on A proceeds alphabetically through seven letter-named pitches to the eighth, the octave, which is A again. (Incidentally, it is not

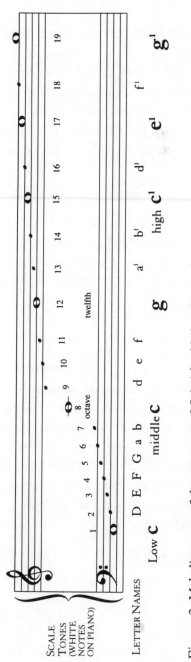

SCALE
TONES
(WHITE
NOTES
ON PIANO)

1 2 3 4 5 6 7 8 9 10 11 12 13 14 15 16 17 18 19

octave   twelfth

LETTER NAMES

Low **C**   **D E F G a b**   middle **C**   **d e f**   **g**   **a¹ b¹**   high **C¹**   **d¹¹**   **e¹**   **f¹**   **g¹**

Figure 2. *Melodic names of the overtones of C (with added scale tones).*

always easy for a child to perceive that a *descending* scale is spelled by reversing the alphabet; why, after all, should down mean backward? But it does. It is difficult for most people to even recite the alphabet backward from G to A. Try it. Unless I'm thinking of musical tones, I can't do it.) Notice that figure 1 is limited to only three of the seven letter names. In figure 2 I have placed the overtones of C in the context of a C-major scale.

Numbers

It is sometimes convenient to use numbers instead of letters. You can begin a scale on any letter A through G and call that letter One. When you play a major scale starting on C, the numbers 1, 2, 3, 4, 5, 6, 7, and 8 correspond to the white keys on the piano (fig. 2).

OCTAVE JUGGLING

Two tones separated by more than an octave are often named as if they were within the same octave. Hence a twelfth becomes—in name—a fifth. Two octaves and a third becomes, simply, a third. Actually doing away with the intervening octaves is called *octave reduction* and allows everything to be easily sung. Although it might make a purist nervous, this process adroitly turns harmonic theory into melodic practice: in real life, melodies usually move by small distances—one or two steps only.

SIMPLE CONFUSION

Thanks to octave reduction, the seminal *harmonic* relationships—3:1 and 5:1—are most often called by their most conve-

	The Whole Rope	Duple Nature	Triple Nature	Quadruple Nature (Duple again)	Pentamerous Nature	Hexamerous Nature (Duple and Triple)
GENERAL USAGE	Generating tone or fundamental	First overtone or first harmonic	Second overtone or second harmonic	Third overtone or third harmonic	Fourth overtone or fourth harmonic	Fifth overtone or fifth harmonic
SCIENTIFIC NAME	First partial	Second partial	Third partial	Fourth partial	Fifth partial	Sixth partial
RATIO WITH C	1:1	2:1	3:1	4:1	5:1	6:1
CYCLES PER SECOND	128	256	384	512	640	768

SCALE TONES (WHITE NOTES ON PIANO): 1 2 3 4 5 6 7 8 9 10 11 12 13 14 15 16 17 18 19

octave — twelfth

LETTER NAMES: Low C — D E F G a b — middle C — d e f — g — a¹ b¹ — high C¹ — d¹ — e¹ — f¹ — g¹

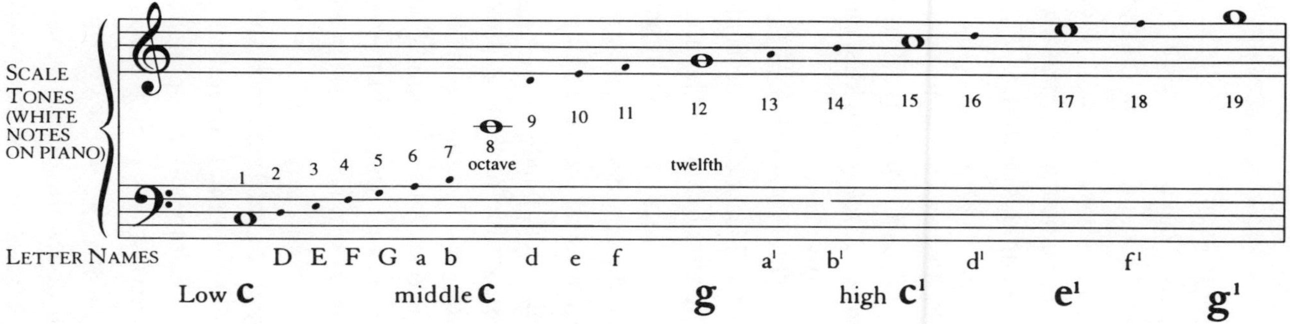

Figure 3. *Harmonic and melodic names together of the overtones of C.*

nient *melodic* names: "fifths" and "thirds." There thus arises
an outrageous embarrassment between melodic and harmonic
names. Looking at figure 3 (which combines figs. 1 and 2),
consider the first G in the overtone series, the "third partial."
Harmonically, it is a 3:1. Melodically, it is a twelfth or, with
the usual octave reduction, a fifth. Any musician will tell you
that C up to G is a fifth.

Now look at the e′, the "fifth partial." Its harmonic name
is 5:1. Its melodic name, with octave reduction, is a third.

Thus a tripling is called a fifth and a quintupling is called
a third. Three is five, kids, and five is three. Time to flunk out
of theory class.

This is the point, in fact, where nearly everyone loses it.
Even well-schooled musicians have rarely clarified this apparent contradiction for themselves. Distinctions between melody
and harmony are typically ignored. So prevalent are the easier,
melodic concepts of distance that the term *interval* has taken
over musical thinking and practice, much to the detriment of
both. Most people learn their way around the musical landscape by the measuring distances only, by interval; and they
think this describes what is going on. It is as if you asked
someone, "How ya doin'?" and instead of hearing, "My girl-
friend came back and I'm soaring," or "The rain is getting me
down," you hear, "Seventeen feet from that rock over there,
and six inches from your nose." Too bad, because clarity
about the relationship between harmonic and melodic space
is precisely what our music once had and has now lost.

Not to cry over anything spilt, but sometimes we need to
retrieve what progress leaves behind. We can't stop walking
because we've learned to fly—we need to feel the earth under
our bones, the fresh basil from the windowbox garden, super-
market or no. The interpenetration of melodic and harmonic

space, the mutuality of their existence, is the quintessence of music. I want us to reclaim this paradigm, to reseed it so it can feed our culture again. We can't let little messy mix-ups between harmonic and melodic nomenclature get in our way.

Three Ways to Produce Overtones

E VERYONE SHOULD HAVE equal access to overtones. Here are three available methods.

METHOD 1

There is a child's toy, that consists of a tube of corrugated plastic about thirty inches long and one and a half inches in diameter, with a two-inch flare at one end. It looks not unlike a vacuum cleaner hose. If the tube is held by the nonflared end and swung around the head, the air flowing over the corrugations sets up standing waves in the tube, just as the circling of your wrist sets up standing waves in the rope during the Rope Trick. A slow-motion circle produces a faint first partial of about 220 cps, which is the A just a little more than an octave below middle C on the piano. A slightly more vigorous spin results in the second partial: the A below middle C. More vigor produces the third partial, the next E; then the fourth partial, the next higher A; then a clean fifth partial, the next C sharp. Almost at the limit will be the sixth partial, the next E. You might be able to coax the seventh partial, a slightly flat G. This is an easy way to climb the overtone ladder.

METHOD 2

A more intimate and musical way of producing the overtone series involves a special kind of singing that places the ladder inside your body instead of outside. You can distinguish the overtones in your own voice if you learn how to bring them forward by resonance. There are various ways of doing this; I will try to describe the most describable and do-able.

First, experiment with putting your speaking voice in your nose. Imitate someone with a colossal nasal twang (no one you know, of course). Next, sing in a normal, nonnasal voice the lowest pitch you can comfortably sing with some power and control. Sing the vowel *oo*, with your lips well forward, making a small opening and a pure vowel sound. Make several such long, low, even tones, breathing deeply for each one.

Next, bring the vowel *very* gradually from *oo* to *uh*, the same *uh* sound you would make if you were playing dumb and saying "duh." That sound is already characteristically nasal, but now put the whole progression strenuously and uncompromisingly in the nose. Raising the back of your tongue a little will help. Also, flare your nostrils.

As your sung vowel shifts *ever so slowly* from nasal *oo* to nasal *uh*, form your lips into the *wh* of why, as though you very much wanted to ask "why," but never could actually get to the sound of the *y* vowel. This will bring the vibration further up into your nose and sinus cavities. You will hear, above your sung tone, a whistle rising in pitch. If you continue the progression of vowels from *uh* to the beginning of *aw*, the whistle may rise higher. Then, as you move back from *aw* through *uh* all the way to *oo* (slowly, slowly, still forming *wh*), the whistle will descend again. While keeping your singing tone strong, well supported, and even, concentrate on the whistle. Its pitch will lie just in the range of your actual whistle, which it will resemble. But when you listen carefully, you will hear that it rises and falls, not like a siren or a teakettle, but according to the discrete quanta of the overtone series. Be patient, move slowly, and listen well.

When you first isolate that terraced whistle in your ear, and then slow down the vowel changes so the individual overtones pop out, you can scarcely believe what you are hearing. Once the whistle is located in your hearing, you can adjust your lips and sinusoidal cavities so as to focus it into a bright silver strand. If you slightly vary the pitch of the sung tone, and then return to the original, it will refocus your hearing. When you have learned to reliably produce the overtones this way, you can also learn to identify the pitches, and make real tunes out of them, especially the higher ones, which lie closer together.

The overtones produced by certain Mongolian singers, who use a technique requiring terrific vocal strength, are so predominant they resemble a high violin. The American David Hykes has produced a number of recordings of choir music based on this more strenuous method.

METHOD 3

A third way to climb the overtonal ladder is to procure a guitar, lay it flat on a table or the floor, and—to be consistent with the nomenclature of this book—tune the third thickest string down from D to C. Keeping the fretboard on your left, use your right index finger to vigorously pluck the now-tuned-to-C string near the bridge of the guitar. Try to hear the composite nature of the sound, scanning it with your ears, bottom to top, and back again. Maybe you hear overtones, maybe not.

Now, perhaps with the aid of a ruler, locate the exact middle of the string, measuring from the nut (that little bridge near the tuning pegs) to the larger bridge below the sound hole. Place your left index finger lightly on that spot—it is the node of the twofold division. With your natural ambidextrous grace, strongly pluck the string with your right finger while leaving your left finger lightly in place. A half second after the pluck, take your left finger away. Taking your finger away too soon will result in too much fundamental, not enough overtone. Leaving it on the string too long will damp both the fundamental and the overtone. With careful touch and timing, you will hear the second partial—middle C—loudly. Experiment until you can balance the fundamental and the overtone so that both are heard clearly at once. Keep in mind that you are not *making* an overtone by touching the node; all the overtones are already fully made when you pluck the string. What you are doing is selectively damping every tone except the one you want to hear.

If you place your left-hand finger exactly one-third of the way along the string (over the twelfth fret) you will hear the third partial, G. This is the clearest partial to hear. Practice until you can reliably produce a ringing G. Now, for the *real* thing, pluck the string without touching it with your left hand: no damping—you get everything at once. Listen through the mass of sound for where the third partial should be. Put your ear there, in the sense of placing your concentration at that pitch.

Of all the moments in a million moments of teaching music, this is my favorite. A person will typically say, "I don't know whether I'm imagining it or whether it's really there." Then, in the comparison back and forth between the enhanced overtone and the merely plucked string, the miracle becomes clear. You used to hear one tone and now there are clearly two, then more; then *more.* Something for nothing. The rose opens. A world within a world. People's faces light up. They hear trumpets, and the light comes shining back through their eyes.

One quarter the length of the string (your left finger lightly over the fifth fret) produces the fourth partial, C.

One-fifth the length (finger over the fourth fret) produces gorgeous, pentamerous E. One-sixth (you find it) produces G. If you experiment, you might be able to produce up to the twelfth partial or beyond.

Of course this whole procedure might be facilitated by asking a guitarist, "Please show me how to produce harmonics on your instrument." None will refuse. Everyone loves that angel light.

You might ask the same favor from a string player (especially a cellist) or any conscious brass player. From French horn players you will almost certainly get a free concert of some length and probably an invitation to dinner.

Overtones are everyday magic, plain as the ears you hear with, yet proof of limitless realms. We need to look for them, and to love them when we find them, and they need to have a loving home in our ears.

String Ocean

H ERE IS ONE of the most affirming practices I know: listening to all the overtones at once.

How can a string, or anything, vibrate at many frequencies simultaneously?

In a tall building, you are riding up and down the elevator. At the same time, you are doing deep knee bends while
greeting a baby with a wave of your wrist. Also, you are shiver-
ing. Your little quick vibrations are nestled within the larger
ones—the shiver inside the greeting inside the knee bends inside the elevator ride—like a set of nested Chinese boxes.

Picture how the tidal fluctuations of the ocean contain
within them the enormous swells; and within those, whale-
size waves, and ripples within those, and foam on the ripples.

Now imagine all those waves at once.

Old joke: Two hippies, leaning on the rail of an ocean
liner, deep in thought.

FIRST HIPPIE: Man, look at all that water.
SECOND HIPPIE: Yeah. (*pause*) And that's only the top.

A string produces all of its waves—its partials—at once,
but most people are aware of only the first partial, which ac-
counts for the lowest and usually the loudest of all the tones.

When you place your finger on the appropriate nodes, you learn to isolate the upper partials, one by one, folding them into your consciousness. Gradually, you practice simply plucking the string and listening for what you know is already there. Hearing two partials at once is a breakthrough, three a celebration. When you know where to look for them, the partials pop out, just as individual speakers will pop out in a roomful of talk. You hear what you want to hear: selective listening. With experience, you hear more and more of the layered sound.

We want to hear everything at once, but this is not an easy want. You have to nurture this want, and hone it, and that is hard work. But the work is worth it. Hearing all the strata of a string tone, from earth to sky, the entire living chord of it, is like sudden fluency in a new language. It is an immediate power that carries over from the specificity of your practice into a heightened awareness of all space. The air is vibrant with messages you did not hear before. You see through the world.

The thicker guitar strings produce the first six partials— the ones we have studied—quite clearly, but there are usually more than a dozen audible ones, climbing up a ladder whose rungs are ever closer together. The tones become fainter as they climb, of course, finally dipping below audibility. Tracking them upward is like climbing out of the top of your head, past the limit of your hearing, past your body, past even this particular act of listening, and into all of listening.

When you climb up out of yourself like that, what changes is not you or the world, but the boundary between: it disappears. Direct harmonic experience vanishes the boundary and makes real—realizes—connectedness. The string ocean becomes your ocean. You are, finally, the site of creation, the very method in its madness, the very beauty it beholds.

Timbre Sauce

I MAGINE THAT EACH OVERTONE has a flavor all its own. The first partial tastes like toasted sesame oil, say, and the second partial like rice vinegar. The third is sake, and on up through miso, garlic, chili oil, fresh ginger, honey. All together, they are a sauce. As you vary the portions of the individual ingredients, you change the taste of the sauce. Likewise, as you vary the loudness of the overtones, you change the quality of the overall sound, the timbre.

The relationship of the tones in the overtone series to one another is the same for every pure tone everywhere. A flute, a clarinet, a violin, and an oboe all playing the same D, for instance, will produce identical overtones, but with different mixtures in the amounts of their loudness. Our ears identify "flute" because we have learned to recognize the flute mixture just as surely as we can recognize Aunt Elizabeth's sesame sauce. Each timbre has an overtone recipe of its own.

As you sing a tone, when you change the vowel you are changing the loudness of the overtones, not the overtones themselves. *Ee* has lots of highs, *oo* cuts the highs and emphasizes the lows; *aah* is more of a balance. In actual speech the mix changes very rapidly. Sometimes, as in the chanting of AUM, you can discern individual little silver rungs of the overtonal ladder as they glisten upward or downward. When people are speaking you can tune in to the quickened aura of sound above their voices. There is a level of meaning above the words, just as there is a deeper level of psychological meaning underlying them; these combine, of course, as one utterance. Every spoken thought has a motive below and a halo above.

Sensitivity to timbre is a little bit like sensitivity to fluctuations of light and shade, color and hue. Doesn't it astonish you how a fractional change in the light can alert your body? Or a whole day will turn on the slightest inflection of a vowel?

The way you said, "I did."

The way she said, "Come on."

The Overtones as Musical Infrastructure

W E DON'T HAVE TO KNOW about ninety-degree angles to see that a building is leaning, or to balance our way across a log bridge. We can know and respond to straight-up-and-down without knowing what we know, or that we know. Even if we have never actually *seen* a perfect ninety-degree angle (who has?), our balance proceeds from the perfect *sense* of the ninety-degree angle our body makes between the center of the earth and the horizon—a built-in norm.

The overtone series presents a built-in norm. Just as our sense of verticality allows us to dance, so our sense of whole-number ratios allows us the intricate playfulness we call music.

Musical harmony isn't driven by overtones. Overtones and music and our ears are all driven by the same innate affinity for duple and triple and quintuple nature. That nature drives music and the ear. It is impossible to separate the ear from what it hears. Meister Eckart says, "The same eye by which I see God is the eye by which God sees me." What we do know is that the ear loves low prime numbers. The house of sound is built from duple and triple and pentamerous events in happy permutation.

I was in deeply into music before I found out how low

prime ratios sit smiling inside its heart. I found out also that such knowledge is not new but lost, or rather, silted over, and I got the call to wash it clean, and raise it from the shallows, and reinterpret it for the present generation. Then I found kindred souls.

Dane Rudhyar, in a book called *The Magic of Tone and Relationship,* says

> The youth who takes guitar, piano, or flute lessons is not aware that there is a problem or a mystery when he speaks of a low C or a high C. He takes for granted that the octave interval is basic, and he never questions why it is so. He even less feels any urge to enquire into the metaphysical and cosmological meaning of the ratio 2:1. Yet any truly basic musical training . . . should start with [I would say, "continuously include"] a meditation on the meaning of the most primary musical relationships. . . . The relationship between the number one and the number two is the great mystery, because it is at the root of all there is; it hides the "why" of existence. If we knew this "why" we would know why a tone seems to us "the same" as its octave, yet obviously different. . . . "God" is the Universal Whole, yet remains . . . transcendent. . . . We can know only his (or its) reflection in the octave sound, the number two of "Being" or rather, "Be-ness."

Most of us are in the same boat as the unaware youth. The proportional elegance of musical harmony is not generally understood, except by academic specialists and a few composers, and certainly not generally taught.

In a few words I can tell you what I know: Virtually all music is made up of low prime ratios, their compounds, their reciprocals, and their approximations.

To *compound* intervals means to stack them; for instance, a doubling of a tripling, or a tripling of a quintupling. Strange as it seems, and as difficult as it is to picture, the wee cleric in the ear knows well how to multiply low prime ratios among themselves.

Reciprocal means that whatever can be multiplied is (almost) as easily divided. It is as if all the notes generated by compounding were lined up on the shore of a deep pond, where their reflections in the water are at least as beautiful as they themselves. The cleric divides and multiplies with the same intelligence.

Approximations figure in because within certain limits and with more or less complaint, the ear accepts what is near to a target as if it were a direct hit. The faster the music, the greater the approximation the ear allows. The slower the music, the longer the ear has to dwell on each tone, the more in tune it had better be. That is one reason why music played on pianos, which are tuned in a highly practical but slightly out-of-tune system, is typically fast-moving.

I say all music is made of low primes, but how low is low? Systems that use only doublings and triplings are called three-limit systems. In most music, quintuplings are usually also in the mix: these are five-limit systems. Western classical music is basically a five-limit system. Some non-Western music makes liberal use of septuplings. These tones—seventh partials—are characteristic of the blues, a spice that has, by now, flavored the whole planet.

Very little music goes beyond the seventh partial. The next prime, eleven, is rare. Thirteen is rarer, and primes higher than thirteen are virtually never used except by composers specializing in increasing the range of our response. Atonal music, which by definition typically avoids the harmony inherent in low primes, is a fascinating but thin sliver of the music pie. Save for exotic flavorings, then, most tonal music uses five-limit as a norm. The vastness of music is encoded in the first few tones of the overtone series.

క

Why so many concepts, and words to explain them? Why read a book *about* music, anyway? All these facts, all these ideas. The truth is I want for them to fall away, for this book to find its way back to the forest, for you to use words to seduce yourself away from them and back to the pure act of listening. That is where your harmonious nature sweeps over you, and leaves your word-mind behind. Then the impeccable cleric in the brain, abacus in hand, turns into a muse, and the interminable clicking of the beads, the immaculate tabulations, are the passing expressions in her eyes.

Our Harmonious Nature

THE THEORY OF QUANTUM MECHANICS changed the way we think. It says, "Being has a price. Marriage means commitment. If you want to marry existence, you have to commit to an energy state." The universe is not a smooth continuum, we are told; it is delivered to us parceled and packaged.

The concept that discrete modes of existence (corresponding to simple integers) lie at the center of everything has given us a terrific way of grasping nature with our minds and understanding ourselves better in the bargain.

What people hear, mostly, when they hear music is how it slips and slides, how it is rounded and roly-poly. But what musicians know is that inside the roundness is always a hard edge: a precise somewhere, not an anywhere. Music is quantized.

I remember the very moment I learned to keep time to music. When I was young my parents sometimes let me listen to the family Philco in my room, to drop me off to sleep. From the somber wooden bell-shaped cabinet glowed a round dial, yellow-orange and flecked with brown numbers. There was a knob in the center you could turn, and a cover of glass fitted over, so you couldn't touch. One night sometime in my third year, just before lights out, my mother came in and sat

on the bed next to me. She said, "Do you know what that is
on the radio? It's Brahms." When she turned off the overhead
light, the dial shone like a moon, and pouring out of it was
Brahms. I didn't know Brahms was a person. Brahms was a
yellow-orange river of sound with chocolate numbers swirling
on top. "Can you clap your hands to it?" asked Mom. I
clapped my hands like applause. She laughed some little bits
of silver into Brahms. "I mean in time to it, like this," and she
took my hands in hers and clapped them in time to the music.
I knew that the clapping belonged somewhere inside the
music, but I didn't know where. "Now do it by yourself," she
said, and I tried, but it didn't fit. She laughed again and turned
the radio low and snuggled me down in the sheets. "I'll show
you tomorrow." I went to sleep with the moon dial making
my white pillow the Brahms color.

The next morning, before anyone else was up, I clicked
on the radio: a pop song on "The Arthur Godfrey Show." I
remember knowing suddenly that I could tap in time to it. So
that's what she meant. What had been a river of sound last
night was now a string of beads. I held still in my cocoon bed,
only my finger tapping, so the new room in my inner world
wouldn't go away.

What I learned then was that meter gives shape to the
river of time, turns it into bricks and slabs—building materials
for musical architecture.

Music didn't have to know it is quantized in order to get
born: it is the soul's spontaneous response to its own nature.
But about 600 BCE the tinkering Pythagoras elegantly related
whole-number ratios to the harmony of the universe. He
showed how musicians play with quantized sound. From the
precise norms of pitch and meter, roundnesses develop like
pearls. At its center music is in tune and in time, but the tune
and the time are not *out there* somewhere. Tune and time are

a reflection of the quantized natural world, a reflection of what it *and* you are made of.

When music is in the air, it and you—outer and inner realms—connect and combine. Even when we get swallowed up by our daily lives, through music we stay in touch with essence. An adolescent who's suffering deeply keeps his circling blackness at bay by connecting with Metallica's back beat through the soles of his feet: duple nature to the rescue.

I stand dripping in the shower, arrested from rescuing my vocalizing wife, laughing because I recognize a major scale. I hear in her voice not fear but playful intelligence. Thanks, she's been rescued already.

A few months ago I was flying high in a jet over Java. All I could see, horizon to horizon, was the quilt of farmers' fields, an eternity of rice, rice growers, and rice eaters. I found myself feeling down: so many people in this world, such an unaccountable sea of beings, how can one possibly begin to sense all of human life—there is too much of it to sense. How can I feel connected if I can't draw a bead on any of it? Believe it or not, I thought of an octave, a 2:1 ratio. Overtones are my worry beads, the certainty I can feel in my sweaty palm when I need something hard and true. An octave is what I know; it is like a functional self. In music, as in number, it is the first limit. Limit has power; it is the first power. Over Java I felt the power of the limit of the octave. It said, "Don't get lost. If you can imagine twoness you can imagine anything. Keep expanding, keep looking. Don't give up on the vision of your mind . . . like any strength, it develops through use. When in doubt, remember me. Trust me."

The mystery of number never goes away. Seeing vibrations and feeling them and singing them will never make solid the bridge between number and feeling. Einstein said he was continually amazed that the numbers he worked with every day had anything to do with the real world. It seems like we must always be laboring to make feeling thinkable and number sensible. But number is nonetheless real.

So real that it realizes us. When we grasp the quantum truth about music we realize that singing in tune isn't just a talent some people have and some people don't. It's not something others do that you can't. Singing in tune is an awareness, infinitely refineable, of something that *is*—is in nature, and in you as a part of nature. You wake up to your nature. Sometimes slowly. Sometimes with a start. Some people seem (to us) to be born awake to music, and maybe some are. But everyone who tries can be awake to it. It's part of the deal.

For me, studying music has been a waking up to sound that has widened into a love of notes so compelling and intimate it seems hard sometimes to differentiate it from other kinds of love. Does love of a friend feel different from love of a major third? Of course. But sometimes, the musical waters flow so deep . . .

In Sanskrit, the name for an in-tune note is a *shruti*. One of the translations of *shruti* is "retold wisdom, transmitted understanding." I love that idea. It means to me that when you sing a note in tune it exists not only in the present but is as old as singing itself, and older, so you can taste all of time when you sing it. Each tone of the scale, sung individually against the drone of the first tone, has its own quality, its own deep face. Each is like a deity hovering in the space. For each we have an individual response. Our appreciation pulls them out of the air and into our lives the same way a goddess hanging around her shrine is realized through the prayers of passersby.

After many caprices and escapades with these beings, they have become my friends. I can count on them for a certain level of give and take, nourishment and difficulty. I know how they mix with each other, whom to invite to the gathering, and whom to politely avoid for the evening. I fancy they like me also, and find me loving and careless by turns. My music deepens as their meaning in my life broadens. They awaken me to my own qualities. In the octave (2:1) I feel certainty. In the perfect fifth (3:2), clarity of mind; in the perfect fourth (4:3), the deepest midnight blue; in the major third (5:4), a calling out of the heart; in the major seventh (15:8), longing; in the minor sixth (6:5), gypsy fire; in the major sixth (5:3), a secret grotto, suffused light and contentment.

As friends will, these friends have their moods, depending on the weather and the company. But they are always friends and always near. They bring me into completion, into my connectedness with the subtle world. They take me past my personal world into a sense of belonging. As well as any humans have, my *shruti* friends have taught me compassion. In loving them, even noise has become more integral to life, because I hear order and meaning where before I heard none.

ℰℐ

The overtone series is a boundary surface between us and everything else. It is an active interface, translating the world to us and, when we are making music, us to the world. It is a teacher within our range of perception and response, our audible teacher whom we can listen to and learn from. Starting here, we extrapolate the existence of an infinity of other teachers, visible and invisible, boundary surfaces we have yet to recognize from experience, subtle interfaces sensed by something in us more sensitive even than the ear. We become very curious about our perceptions, about other kinds of numbers, and what someday may be revealed.

Because the specificity of quantum consciousness concretizes the universe for us, forms it, it gives us a purchase on the void. The thrown rope that rescues us from the ocean of infinity turns out to be a jump rope dividing neatly into prime-number frequency ratios. Form from void. Saved again.

Spinoza said that mathematics is the music of the soul; we might as easily say that music and number are soul mates. If we could get a clear picture of how numbers reflect reality, we might understand how music reflects reality. We might understand reflection itself—it's all done with mirrors, and we've scarcely a clue. My thinking today, at 10:15 P.M., listening to the crickets on my farm under a waxing moon: The overtone series doesn't clarify anything for us. It doesn't signify anything. What it does is deepen experience. It deepens what is. It is a way of entering the inside and outside realms, a swinging gate. We are not a vessel for music. It doesn't really go through us. It is our essence itself, realized. It is what we are when we are whole. When we are sound.

8

Honeysuckle Breath

World Craziness

A COLUMNIST, SUSAN SWARTZ, wrote recently from Germany: "The noise that women are capable of making over Bosnia is not something that sounds like crying. Nor would it be the small strangled noises that come from the throat of someone paralyzed with fear. It could be a great roar, a terrible thundering. It's a sound we know. It's the one we practice over and over in self-defense classes. It comes from the belly, up from the center and out, and is louder than the beast's."

Since you are reading this book, the chances are that you have the time to think about the quality of your life and its musical nature and to envision a harmonious future. For most of us it is impossible to consider these things without feeling the pangs of craziness in the world beyond these pages, beyond our friends and social borders, beyond our good food and rich culture. The pangs can drain us with guilt or inspire us to righteous action, or both; usually they burn unquietly blue as we drive from work to mall to doctor and home again.

Most of us readers are incomprehensibly privileged by being born when and where we are. To feel the African hunger, the violent anxiety of the Balkans, the poverty just outside the window—what to do with the hurt of the world? Of course each person responds uniquely to the inequalities of life; my

213

response, tangled as it is, always comes down to the recognition that I have to begin with my own harmony. To some it may seem like a monstrous act of ego to say, "If I take a calm breath and sing a gentle note I am an instrument for a peaceful world." But this point of view need not be egocentric. What makes it sensible and true is the practice of calm breathing and gentle singing. The question is not, How could little old me save the world? "Little old me" is the ego talking. The question is, How can I be whole now, in this moment?

If you are whole in your sound, your wholeness does not stop with your skin. Sound is sympathetic. The sound of your body is sympathetic with other bodies. All around the globe, incantations for peace as well as cries of outrage are heard and felt. Joining your voice to the voices of others lifts it up to a great circle of sympathetic vibration. The more of yourself you put into your sound the more of you will be in the circle. When you can find your integrity in your voice, when it is real for you, your one centered sound centers everyone. The more you tune it, the more it tunes the world. In one clear tone there is that much sanity.

As If It Were Music

I USED TO BE WARY of religious altars, especially in poor
neighborhoods and impoverished countries. Amid sewage
and deprivation one finds gold-covered naves, daises of precious stones, the stored craft and labor of generations. Why
not spread the wealth? I thought. Gradually, though, I have
realized how it is that altars arise from the poor. They arise
from the rich also. They arise from within our bodies. An altar
is a metaphor for consciousness. Now I see how necessary it is
to discriminate the empowering from the disabling, the gener-
ative from the sterilizing, the stuff that makes you feel OK
from the stuff that brings you down. Over here in this part of
the room I'll put the rock from the garden where Jacqueline
kissed me when we were eight, the snapshot from Lucy's sixth
birthday party, the "honey" card from Devi, the music box
from Thailand that made me cry, the red cord Guruji tied
around my wrist. Just as in a Peruvian village, my altar stands
against the pallor and defilement of the world.

Music makes an altar out of our ears. A single struck
tone, a note blown from a flute, can flush the body with
goodness.

If you strike or pluck the string of a piano, guitar, or harp
and listen to it deeply all the way past its own disappearance,
you'll notice how a musical tone relaxes the defenses. It's as if

the sound promises that nothing bad will happen in church. You open up. The periodicity in the tone gives permission to seek beauty and order everywhere. Then as the tone gets softer you become increasingly aware of the sounds around you. The moment in the tone's decay when the ambient sounds in the environment catch up with it is fascinating. Concentration on this boundary gives life a glow. It is a great teacher. As you pass from the sound of the tone to the sound of the world, if you don't let your ears change attitude, you can keep your altar in place. You'll hear the sounds around you with the same attraction, hear the world as if it were music. It is the love of sound itself that makes an altar out of your ears, just as love of the world makes each place—glistening sand and broken pavement—an altar.

Leaving your ears open like this is immensely fulfilling, but leaving them open *and* unattended is not prudent. Loud sounds can hurt you; sometimes the world does bite. Altars need protection. But once you know that the goodness of music can enter into your everyday hearing by listening to your life as if it were music, you become a walking altar and your ears a holy space.

Honeysuckle Breath

THIS SPRING WAS one long scent of honeysuckle. Our little hedge blooms in late April. Every year the first whiff of the first blossom is a euphoric zoom to childhood, where they keep the best honeysuckle that ever was. This year the ritual was more than a treat. Standing by the hedge, inhaling the perfume, I was swept by a longing for life to always be this way. Ten long breaths, twenty breaths, the pleasure did not fade. Why can't every breath in life be an ecstatic completion?

Once before, in early adolescence, I had seriously posed this question to myself: If orgasm feels so good, so right and complete, why can't we have one all the time? This is a childish question, of course, you say and I say; life is not like that one little bit. Yet standing smelling the honeysuckle I remembered well the thirteen-year-old who asked metaphysically and seriously, If you were God wouldn't you fix it so that we felt fantastic all the time, no let-downs? And now I was asking this again: why not?

And now I am asking you: why not?

The implicit expectation we have from the music we love is that each moment be filled with good feeling, something that will lead us on to the next good-feeling moment. Joyful music is like breathing honeysuckle: high as a kite in every beat. A truly wonderful piece is continuous affirmation. The ears never stop saying "delicious, delicious . . ." Childish as it may seem from one point of view, an ecstatic piece of music does address directly the desire for prolonged ecstasy, and in a safe, public, and collective way, it delivers the goods.

It is part of growing up to recognize innocent desire, to own it and inhabit it willfully. Then we can transform it into something useful. Music is an agent for that recognition. In the safe haven of music, we can live in our pleasure shame-lessly, intelligently, experimentally, indulgently. We can take hours—years—to learn that part of our nature.

And then we can stop the music. If we have learned music's lesson, we don't need it anymore. We plain *outgrow* it, at least for a while. Music can take you to the place beyond the need for music.

This is the real meaning of the musical life—to live and breathe musically with the intense pleasure and satisfaction that music can give, but without music per se. Having gone through the evolutionary spiral of music, we can return to the source. We have emerged from the hollow log drum and the two-step and the fugue. Having been through music, we can live both before and beyond it. The deep moment of music listening when we are utterly receptive, when we feel the thrill of allowing into our bodies all that is heard—that moment can be the norm of everyday living.

"Breathe in joy and breathe out joy," Sufi Sam said—the best teaching I was ever given. Real holy folks show you this; you see it and feel it. They are not singing or conducting or composing, they are breathing in joy and breathing out joy. Honeysuckle breath without the honeysuckle.

Music can take you past itself to a refined place where the hunger for music, the lust of the ear, is observed as a kind of separate thing, a civilized discontent. From such a vantage point the music hunger subsides and light arises. The very air is a surfeit, an enveloping feast. Being completes itself without conditions. Cosmic harmony—the sound of exultation beyond the form of either trumpet or prophet—is all there is. Although musical forms do come to us and hundreds of doors do swing open, when the forms are transcended, "this *praising sound* floods the world."

But then softly, from down the street, the sweet keening of a violin, and we remember our lost loves and our hearts beat again, and music rushes back through the whole neighborhood. Amazingly, this is not a coming-down. It is a living-out. We live poised like this between the love of music and the freedom from it, where any move is true.

Sources and Diversions

PART 1: LIFE MUSIC

Shower Hero

Page 3: "... civilized by tone and tune." I am borrowing from seventeenth-century English author Thomas Fuller's description of music as "nothing else but wild sounds civilized into time and tune."

Bug on a Tamboura

Page 10: "... by slowing down a tape recording . . ."—which is, of course, what I did. So incredibly tonal are the calls of the Swainson's thrush that I was moved to reply with my own pianistic responses, and an excerpt from this conversation is in a piece of mine called *Slow Motion Thrush* (1985).

Page 11: "Devi says . . .": Devi subsequently wrote: "I've since discovered this is the Boxelder Bug, *Leptcoris trivittatis,* which likes to hibernate indoors in winter. I guess we notice them in spring when hidden hibernators emerge. They are harmless to plants and household stuff."

Electric Bridge

Page 19: "Garland Hirschi's Cows": The cassette is available from Phillip Kent Bimstein, P.O. Box 301, Springdale, UT 84767.

Page 11: Martin Swan's quote is from *Keyboard* magazine, June 1991.

First World Piece

Page 21: "Symphony of Place": A chapter in my first book, *The Listening Book* (Shambhala, 1991), is devoted to Symphonies of Place. A week after it was published I discovered a book called *The Third Ear: On Listening to the World* (Element Books) by Joachim-Ernst Berendt, written in 1985 and translated from the German in 1988. It is a comprehensive if peripatetic book and not a little polemical: he wants us to understand how visual sensibilities have usurped and eclipsed aural ones. But in the midst of his argument, in a chapter called "Landscapes of the Ear: A Summer Experience," is a warm, deeply observed chronicle of five hours of listening on the shore of a mountain lake in Oregon. I was charmed at first, then chagrined to find I had stolen someone's thunder, so to speak, without knowing it; but then I began to enjoy the synchronicity. There *is*, generally, a rekindled awareness of listening, and I'm glad that many people are talking about it in various ways. An earlier book by the same author is *Nada Brahma: The World Is Sound: Music and the Landscape of Consciousness* (Destiny Books, 1987).

On the other hand, I have known about the writings of R. Murray Schafer for some time. In "The Music of the Environment," an essay included in *Cultures I* (UNESCO, 1973), Schafer's passionate sense of hearing can be felt through the page; his very fine book *The Soundscape: Our Sonic Environment and the Tuning of the World* (Destiny Books, 1994) came directly from this work. I've been gladly influenced by Schafer's language and thought; the equivalent, in sound, of sightseeing is his idea. Here is one good sentence: "Just as the sewing machine gave us the long line in clothes, the motor gave us the flat line in sound." In discussing the invention of the loudspeaker he says, "We have split the sound from the maker of the sound. Sounds have been torn from their natural sockets and given an amplified and independent existence. Vocal sound, for instance, is no longer tied to a hole in the head but is free to issue from anywhere in the landscape." For this condition he invents the word *schizophonia*.

PART 2: MUSIC AND WORDS

Music versus Words

Page 29: Joe Miller died in 1992. A new book, *Great Song: The Life and Teachings of Joe Miller,* by Richard Power, with a foreword by Coleman Barks, is available from Maypop Books, 191 E. Broad St., Suite 202, Athens, GA 30601.

Page 30: "Enough talking . . .": All of the Rumi poems quoted in this book are from versions by Coleman Barks and used with his permission. The first five quoted here are ending lines of poems from *Open Secret* (pages 29, 28, 31, 32, 50); likewise "If I could wake . . ." (page 41) and "You know this already" (page 30). "A mouth . . ." is from *Like This* (page 13) and "I used to want . . ." is from *We Are Three* (page 14). When I first read *Open Secret* I went into ecstasy not because of Rumi (whom I had read in other translations) but because of Barks. As a composer, I had been looking my entire life for meaningful poetry that sings itself, and had come up mostly empty. Now suddenly here was a *book* of song cycles. I began to compose what I knew would become a life's work: vocal settings of Coleman's extraordinarily musical Rumi. Ten years and many songs later my opinion hasn't changed. And I seem to be one of a growing throng similarly affected. A catalog of his works is available from the address in the preceding note.

Listening to Evening

Page 33: "When the evening . . ." is from T. S. Eliot's "The Love Song of J. Alfred Prufrock." Used courtesy of Faber and Faber Ltd.

Page 33: ". . . metaphor and simile . . .": No writer has better shown me the ubiquity of figurative language than Anne Eisenberg in her essay "Metaphor in the Language of Science" (*Scientific American,* May 1992, p. 144). *Muscle* comes from "little mouse," *bacteria* from "little staffs."

PART 3: SOUND SELF

Sound Apples

Page 50: ". . . a homonym . . .": Friends who live on Puget or Long Island Sound may know that *sund* in German means "straight." *Sound* is actually a three-way homonym.

Page 50: ". . . the Latin *sonare* . . .": Sound, in the meaning derived from *sonare,* "to make noise," has three aspects, and the meaning is not complete unless all three are clear. "A tree falls in the forest but no one hears it—is there a sound?" plays with the lack of clarity in our general usage of the word. In its complete sense, sound needs:

1. A source, usually a body of matter that vibrates, like a mockingbird's syrinx.

2. A medium. Matter is needed to propagate sound waves outward. The medium can be solid (railroad tracks), liquid (chicken soup), or gaseous (nitrogen), as long as there are sufficient molecules to transmit the shape of the vibrations. No medium, no transmission. Sometimes perturbations in the medium itself function as the source, as the airy vortices in wind whistling around the corner, or a flute.

3. An ear to hear. The medium touches the stretched membrane of the eardrum. Our brain registers the vibration. Some of what the brain registers, or all of it, or none of it, then becomes conscious. The degree and quality of consciousness conditions our response. A child impassively hears a sound (squealing brakes), stores it in memory, and forgets about it. Thirty years later, another sound activates the forgotten one, which results this time in an emotional response (she weeps). Is the delayed reaction part of the original sound? You could say that. It took thirty years for the sound to be fully heard. The answer to "what is the sound of one hand clapping?" becomes a matter of how inclusive your definition of sound is. A single hand waving in air makes a vibration too slow for humans to register through their ears, although a large beast might indeed hear it. Does this take the fun out of the koan? Not really. The subject of the koan is the perfidy of linguistic terms. Any vibration is potentially sound, including what we imagine we hear. We can say, "In the beginning was sound," and, "The world is sound," if we sufficiently stretch the common physical dimensions of the definition. If an intelligence pervades the universe, then mind can be thought of as a medium for vibration; any event in time is vibratory. Name your sound. Name your music.

Sound Memory

Page 53: ". . . tell their own stories." Now that I've told you some of my sound stories, if you'd like to tell me some of yours, I'd love to hear them. And if it's OK to publish your stories, let me know that too—wouldn't a collection of them be fascinating?

Breathing Sound

Page 63: *Zen Flesh, Zen Bones* (Charles E. Tuttle), an elegant collection of Zen and pre-Zen writings transcribed by Nyogen Senzaki and Paul Reps, is a lot of people's favorite book, and right up there on my Very Short List. It may have done more than any other book to open Westerners to the practicality and beauty of Zen Buddhism. The quoted phrase is from Number 2 in a series of 112 brief practices called "Centering" (page 193).

Ultimate Mixer

Page 65: ". . . to take responsibility . . .": When enough individuals take responsibility for the sounds in their lives, they instigate collective action, of which noise abatement laws are an example. The city of San Jose, California, I hear on the news this morning, has imposed a fine of forty-eight dollars if the police have to come to your house more than once for a "loud music response." We are still a people of great hope.

PART 4: THE MUSIC MIRROR

Some Music Mirrors

Page 73: ". . . harmonious society . . .": Let me recommend the piano concertos of Mozart from No. 12 and later (through the twenty-seven he wrote), and any by Beethoven, Schumann (there's only one), Brahms, or Prokofiev. The list goes on from there and includes concertos not only for the piano but virtually every orchestral instrument, especially the violin. Antonio Vivaldi, in the first half of the eighteenth century, when the implicit metaphor of the concerto form was youthfully energetic in Europe, wrote five hundred of them. I am indebted to Richard Taruskin for his essay "Vivaldi's Music: A Vital Link" (*Musical Heritage Review,* November 1991), in which he speaks of "soundly organized humanity." He compares the atmosphere at a performance of a new Vivaldi concerto with that of a jazz band in the heyday of swing: "animal spirits, exuberant virtuosity, relentless drive, and probably a noisy, enthusiastic audience."

Home

Page 79: "The search for home . . .": Why has the homing instinct developed so keenly in tonal music? My hunch is that it is a refinement of the survival mechanism that allows us to read the languages of the animals and the elements, and thus identify our coordinates in the natural world. To stay alive we have to recognize where we are, and who is there with us.

PART 5: WHAT A COMPOSER DOES

Craft

Page 107: ". . . scratch their heads . . .": Tedd Judd, a Seattle neuropsychologist, in comparing throughcomposed music (performed for passive listeners) with central, participatory experience (such as music once was) says, "Music was not originally intended to say 'I felt joy once and it was like this,' but 'Let's party!' Not 'I felt grief once,' but 'We are grieving together.' Not 'I prayed once,' but 'Let us pray' " (*Boston Globe*, page 24, November 23, 1992).

What Is It a Piece Of?

Page 112: *Microcosmos* (Touchstone, 1991) made me realize how much you can say about the universe by saying one thing well.

Writing It

Page 121: ". . . trying to sing . . .": This often-told anecdote about Charlie Parker was reenacted brilliantly in the movie *Bird*, directed by Clint Eastwood.

Pleasure in the Long Cycle

Page 123: *Ten Bulls:* My source is *Zen Flesh, Zen Bones*, cited above (notes to Part 3). The pictures and the verses that accompany them were done originally in the twelfth century by the Chinese master Kakuan; these were based on earlier Taoist bulls, called oxherding pictures, of which there were only eight. The illustrations in *Zen Flesh, Zen Bones* are by the contemporary woodblock artist Tomikichiro Tokuriki.

Fighting the Dead

Page 130: ". . . and remain jealous of him." This is one among numerous flaws in *Amadeus*. As played in the movie, Salieri's love of Mozart was just as intense and clear as his hatred. I find this implausible because if you *really* hear him you can't *really* hate him. Historically it is known that Salieri did not poison Mozart, but the myth grew and persists even now, as though it were part of our collective will, a gossipy little way we have of projecting our jealousies.

So That's What We Do

Page 134: the "treasure book about them" is Paul Berliner's *The Soul of Mbira: Music and Traditions of the Shona People of Zimbabwe* (University of Chicago Press, 1993, hardcover and paper). Aside from a detailed description of the music, the book chronicles the author's absorbtion of the tradition and treats with delicacy and compassion the crucial contemporary subject of transmitting the music of a culture beyond its boundaries. The same considerations are applied to jazz in his most recent book, *Thinking in Jazz: The Infinite Art of Improvisation* (University of Chicago Press, 1994, paper). As an introduction to Shona mbira music I recommend two Nonesuch albums: *The Soul of Mbira* (H-72054) and *Shona Mbira Music* (H-72077).

PART 6: SOUND IS THE TEACHER

Abundance

Page 139: ". . . roaming inside the powers of ten . . .": Philip Morrison's *The Powers of Ten: A Book about the Relative Size of Things in the Universe and the Effect of Adding Another Zero* (Scientific American Library, 1982) shuttles you between micro- and macroworlds in about forty increments with dynamite illustrations, and is a wonderful way to get a fix on your place in the cosmos. There is also a companion film (or video) I've never seen (am I born too late?) that is supposed to be terrific. The idea comes from an earlier book from Holland called *The Universe in Forty Jumps.*

Page 139: "Please tell me where I am . . .": As this book was being prepared for publication I came across an interview with the philosopher Paul Karl Feyerabend in *Scientific*

American (May 1993), whose current book-in-progress has the working title *The Conquest of Abundance*. "The world is really abundant," he says, "and all enterprises consist in cutting down this abundance. First of all, the perceptual system cuts it down or you couldn't survive." Singing in tune might thus be thought of as a way of "cutting down the abundance." "Philosophers and scientists," Feyerabend goes on to say, "cut it down further."

Firefly Constellations

Page 144: I have taken this description of the firefly phenomenon largely from a *Science News* article, "Step in Time: Exploring the Mathematics of Synchronously Flashing Fireflies" (vol. 140, no. 9, August 31, 1991).

Octave Mystery

Page 155: ". . . two ways to answer . . .": The model of a corkscrew, or coil, is often given as one answer, with the spiraling ramp of the Guggenheim Museum in Manhattan as a reference. When you walk around the ramp one full revolution, you are at the same place in the circular dimension, but higher in the vertical. This seems to work until you ask what is the analogue of the circular dimension in the act of hearing. And you are left with the question "What is it that stays the same?" still begging. The most feasible theories (to me) emphasize the hookups and functions of the auditory nerves themselves.

PART 7: SOUND IS THE TEACHER

Triple Nature

Page 171: My source for the Lao-tsu quote (and the Kepler quote in "Pentamerous Nature") is *Tone: A Study in Musi-*

cal Acoustics by Siegmund Levarie and Ernst Levy (Kent State University Press, 1980), a book which gives me more real answers to more real questions than any other I've read about the reciprocity between music and the ear.

A House for Sound

Page 174: The ethnomusicologist David Reck put the question "What is music?" to a group of children. One freckle-faced girl responded, "Music is the house that sound lives in." This anecdote (on page 403), along with a few thousand other observations, pictures, and insightful articulations, are in Mr. Reck's *Music of the Whole Earth* (Scribners, 1977), a truly global tour.

Pentamerous Nature

Page 179: The Kepler passage has been translated from the German by the authors of *Tone* (see the entry above the entry above). In the original work, Kepler compares the vital power of pentamerous plants to the frozen structure of hexagonal snowflakes.

Three Ways to Produce Overtones

Page 194: ". . . move slowly . . .": Another version of this method is presented in Kay Gardner's *Sounding the Inner Landscape: Music as Medicine* (Caduceus, 1990), page 69.

Page 194: "David Hykes has produced a number of recordings . . .": Among them are *David Hykes and the Harmonic Choir: Harmonic Meetings* (Celestial Harmonies 013/14) and *Windhorse Riders* (with Djamchid Chemirani; New Albion 024).

The Overtones as Musical Infrastructure

Page 202: Dane Rudhyar was a wild, learned astrologer-composer. *The Magic of Tone and Relationship* (Shambhala,

1982), a hoary metaphysical ramble laced with clear prophecy, is extremely out of print. I know because I did a computer search and couldn't find a single copy. My friends at Shambhala couldn't find one either. My source is the proofreader's prepublication copy given to me by the author in 1981. Mostly what I got from the book was Rudhyar's clear-channel passion. He showed me how he lived through the emotions in his ideas.

Page 202: ". . . a few composers . . .": Well known among them are Lou Harrison and Harry Partch. *Lou Harrison's Music Primer* features impeccable calligraphy (by Ron Pendergraft), a pastiche of items concerning ratio and tone, and gentle wisdom from the center as well as the edges of musical composition. One entry: "It seems to me that children—when they come to fractions in their study of mathematics—ought to be allowed to tune these relationships; &, too, that they certainly might well learn the ratios for at least the two commonest modes of their own culture." The book is available from C. F. Peters, 373 Park Ave. South, New York, New York 10016. Another composer's book, which has become a classic, is Harry Partch's *Genesis of a Music* (Da Capo Press, New York, 1949). I would also like to acknowledge the work of Paul Boomsliter and Warren Creel, whose unpublished manuscripts came to me from unseen hands. One of them has been photocopied so many times that the title page can hardly be read, but here it is: *Interim Report On the Project On* (this penciled in) *Tuning* (then big letters) *ORGANIZATION IN AUDITORY PERCEPTION* (now modest little caps) AT THE STATE UNIVERSITY COLLEGE, ALBANY NEW YORK (February 1962). When I first saw this paper, in 1972, I was formulating my understanding of music, number, and soul, but from an academic point of view, I was a crazed hippie, all over the map. The precise language and clear procedures of these two gentlemen sobered me up. They were the first, I think, to really understand and articulate the ancient, modal roots of modulating tonality (our kind of music), and they gave me the courage to write about what I deeply hear.

Our Harmonious Nature

Page 207: ". . . it *and* you . . .": A German hydrodynamics engineer named Theodor Schwenk was not only an observant scientist but also a student of the spiritual science of Rudolf Steiner. After spending a life "watching water and air with unprejudiced eyes," he came to a changed understanding of what is alive. His book *Sensitive Chaos* (Rudolf Steiner Press, softcover, available from The Rudolf Steiner College Bookstore, 9200 Fair Oaks Blvd., Fair Oaks, California 95628) was for me a great opening into the reciprocity of nature and sensibility, water and fish, sound and the ear. He led me to appreciate as well the creativity that exists at boundary surfaces. There are superbly chosen photographs comparing, for instance, the forms of water vortices with the forms of sea shells. This is one of those hidden classics that you can't understand why everybody hasn't read.

PART 8: HONEYSUCKLE BREATH

World Craziness

Page 213: Susan Swartz is quoted with permission from the *Santa Rosa* (California) *Press Democrat*, January 24, 1993.

Honeysuckle Breath

Page 218: ". . . both before and beyond it . . .": In the early years of the twentieth century, Inayat Khan gave up an extraordinary career as a North Indian musician to become a teacher of Sufism, the first from the East to face the Western world head on. Partly as a consequence of his musical depth and training, he found a way of articulating, with clarity and enormous scope, the mystic's love of essence. He was acutely aware that he was not practicing his vina ten hours a day, but rather writing and lecturing and traveling and teaching, showing the world with endless patience the nature of his beloved Beloved. He died young, at forty-two, in 1927. *The Music of Life* (Omega Press, 1983) is a collection of his writings particularly informed by the knowledge of vibration. In a chapter called "Spiritual Development by the Aid of Music" he refers to music as the bridge between form and the formless (page 134). In a chapter called "The Word That Was Lost" (page 67) he says, "The difference between the mystical and the scientific point of view is this, that the scientist says that from the rock intelligence developed by a gradual process, whereas the mystic says that the rock was only a grade of intelligence; intelligence was first, and the rock came afterwards." This book more than any other has deepened and quickened the musical quality of my life.

Page 219: ". . . and hundreds of doors . . ." is adapted from the Rumi poem on page 27 of *Like This,* versions by Coleman Barks (Maypop, 1990).

Discography

SOLO PIANO ALBUMS BY W. A. MATHIEU

Streaming Wisdom (1981)   *Available Light* (1987)
In the Wind (1983)   *Celebration* (1990)
Second Nature (1985)   *Lakes and Streams* (1991)
Listening to Evening (1986)

MUSICAL SETTINGS OF THE POEMS OF RUMI

In the Arc of Your Mallet/Quatrains (1988). Text translated by Coleman Barks. Composed by W. A. Mathieu. Sung by Devi Mathieu and members of the Sufi Choir, with W. A. Mathieu, piano.

The Sufi Choir Jubilee Album (1994). A collection of favorites from previous releases of the Sufi Choir. Music composed and directed by W. A. Mathieu.

A complete catalogue is available from:

Cold Mountain Music
P.O. Box 912
Sebastopol, CA 95473